Mobile App Development with Flutter: Build Cross-Platform Apps

A Step-by-Step Guide to Mastering Mobile App Development with Flutter

BOOZMAN RICHARD

BOOKER BLUNT

Table of Content

TABLE OF CONTENTS

INTRODUCTION 11

Mastering Flutter: A Comprehensive Guide to Building Cross-Platform Apps 11

Why Flutter? 11

What This Book Covers 12

Why This Book is Essential 14

Who This Book is For 15

Why Learn Flutter? 16

Conclusion 16

Chapter 1 18

Getting Started with Flutter 18

Chapter 2 27

Dart Language Basics 27

Chapter 3 36

Flutter Widgets: The Building Blocks 36

Chapter 4 50

Building Layouts with Flutter 50

Chapter 5 62

Flutter Navigation and Routing 62

Key Concepts in Navigation: 62

Pushing a Screen (Navigating Forward): 63

Popping a Screen (Navigating Back): 64

Passing Data through Constructors: 64

- Defining Named Routes: 66
- Navigating with Named Routes: 67
- Passing Arguments with Named Routes: 67
- Step 1: Defining the Screens 69
- Step 2: Navigating Between Screens 71
- Step 3: Retrieving Data in the Second Screen 71

Chapter 6 73

Working with User Input 73

Chapter 7 87

Styling Your App 87

- Material Widgets: 93

Chapter 8 101

Managing App State 101

- How InheritedWidget Works: 107

Chapter 9 116

Working with External Libraries 116

- Steps to Add Dependencies: 117

Chapter 10 126

Making Your App Interactive 126

- How it works: 130
- Using AnimationController: 133
- Step 1: Define the Animation: 135
- Step 2: Explanation of the Code: 137

Chapter 11 139

Networking in Flutter 139

- Making a GET Request 140
- Making a POST Request 141

Parsing JSON into Dart Objects........143
Handling HTTP Errors........145
Explanation:........151
Chapter 12........153
Local Storage in Flutter........153
Storing Data with SharedPreferences........154
Retrieving Data from SharedPreferences........155
Removing Data........156
Creating the SQLite Database........157
Inserting Data into SQLite........159
Querying Data from SQLite........160
Updating and Deleting Data........160
Explanation of the Code:........165
Chapter 13........167
Using Firebase with Flutter........167
Steps to Set Up Firebase:........168
Setting Up Firebase Authentication:........171
Setting Up Firestore:........175
Using Firestore:........175
Retrieving Data from Firestore:........176
Listening for Real-Time Updates:........177
Explanation:........182
Chapter 14........184
Flutter and Device Features........184
Using the Camera Plugin........184
Using the Image Picker Plugin........187
Chapter 15........200

Handling Notifications in Flutter 200

- Steps to Set Up FCM: 201
- Steps to Set Up Local Notifications: 206

Chapter 16 217

Testing Your Flutter App 217

- Unit Tests 218
- Widget Tests 220
- Using Flutter DevTools for Debugging: 223
- Step 1: Build the Counter App 224
- Step 2: Write Unit Tests for the Counter App 226
- Step 3: Write Widget Tests for the Counter App 227

Chapter 17 230

Debugging and Performance Optimization 230

- Key Features of Flutter DevTools: 230
- Setting Up DevTools: 231
- Common Performance Bottlenecks: 232
- Using the Performance View in DevTools: 232
- Optimizing Frame Rendering: 233
- Optimizing Startup Time: 234
- Optimizing Memory Usage: 235
- Step 1: Build a Simple App 236
- Step 2: Debugging Performance with DevTools 237
- Step 3: Optimize the Code 238

Chapter 18 241

Deploying Your App to the App Stores 241

- Steps to prepare your app for iOS deployment: 241
- Steps to prepare your app for Android deployment: 242

1. App Icons: 244

2. Splash Screens: 245

1. Publishing to the Google Play Store: 247

2. Publishing to the Apple App Store: 248

1. Versioning: 249

2. Handling App Updates: 250

Chapter 19 253

Flutter for Web and Desktop Apps 253

Advantages of Flutter for Web: 253

Steps to Set Up Flutter for Web: 254

Key Techniques for Building Responsive Web UIs: 256

Setting Up Flutter for Desktop: 259

Step 1: Create a New Flutter Project 260

Step 2: Modify the UI for Web and Desktop 261

Step 3: Make the App Responsive 262

Step 4: Run on Multiple Platforms 264

Step 5: Build for Multiple Platforms 264

Chapter 20 266

Integrating with Third-Party Services 266

Making REST API Calls in Flutter: 266

Steps to Use REST APIs in Flutter: 266

Steps to Integrate Payment Gateways in Flutter: 270

Steps to Integrate Firebase Analytics: 273

Step 1: Set Up Stripe: 275

Step 2: Add Stripe Dependencies: 276

Step 3: Initialize Stripe: 276

Step 4: Implement Payment Flow: 277

Step 5: Backend Setup for Payment Intent: 278

Chapter 21 281

Using Advanced Flutter Widgets 281

Why Create Custom Widgets? 281

Creating a Simple Custom Widget 281

StatefulWidget Basics 283

Example: A Counter Widget 284

StatefulWidget Lifecycle 286

Using CustomPainter 286

Example: Drawing a Circle 287

CustomPainter Use Cases 288

Step 1: Define the CustomPainter 289

Step 2: Use CustomPainter in a Widget 291

Explanation: 292

Chapter 22 294

Advanced State Management Solutions 294

Provider: The Flutter State Management Library 294

Riverpod: A More Robust Provider Alternative 298

BLoC (Business Logic Component) Architecture 301

How BLoC Works: 301

Setting Up BLoC: 302

How Redux Works: 305

Setting Up Redux: 306

Chapter 23 312

Advanced Animations in Flutter 312

Key Concepts: 312

Explanation: 315

Using Implicit Curves 316
Creating Custom Curves 317
Explanation of Custom Curves: 318
Using PageRouteBuilder for Custom Screen Transitions 318
Using AnimatedSwitcher for UI Element Transitions 320
Step 1: Define the Profile Screen Layout 321
Step 2: Explanation 324
Chapter 24 326
Security in Flutter Apps 326
Why is Security Important in Flutter Apps? 326
JWT (JSON Web Token) Authentication 327
Using JWT in Requests: 329
OAuth Authentication 330
OAuth with Google: 330
Setting Up Secure Storage: 332
How Secure Storage Works: 334
Step 1: Set Up the App UI 334
Step 2: Implementing the Login Functionality 337
Step 3: Securely Storing the Token 338
Step 4: Accessing the Token 339
Chapter 25 341
Building Multi-language (Internationalized) Apps 341
What is Internationalization (i18n)? 341
What is Localization (l10n)? 342
Steps to Set Up Localization in Flutter: 343
Formatting Date and Time: 347
Handling Currency: 348

Handling Numbers: 349

Step 1: Create Translation Files 350

Step 2: Implement the App UI 351

Explanation: 354

Chapter 26 356

Maintaining and Scaling Flutter Apps 356

Key Strategies for Scaling Flutter Apps: 356

Offline Support in Flutter: 358

Setting Up CI/CD for Flutter Apps: 361

Step 1: Optimize the UI: 363

Step 2: Implement Offline Support: 364

Step 3: CI/CD Setup: 364

Step 4: Load Balancing and Backend Scaling: 365

Chapter 27 367

The Future of Flutter and Mobile App Development 367

Upcoming Features in Flutter: 367

Key Trends in Mobile App Development: 369

Why Choose Flutter for PWAs? 371

Steps to Create a PWA with Flutter: 372

Steps Involved: 375

INTRODUCTION

Mastering Flutter: A Comprehensive Guide to Building Cross-Platform Apps

In today's fast-paced world of mobile and web development, developers are constantly searching for efficient, reliable, and powerful tools to create high-performance applications. Flutter, Google's open-source UI toolkit, has rapidly emerged as one of the most popular solutions for building natively compiled applications for mobile, web, and desktop from a single codebase. **"Mastering Flutter: A Comprehensive Guide to Building Cross-Platform Apps"** is designed to help developers—from beginners to experts—master the art of building sophisticated, feature-rich cross-platform apps using Flutter.

Why Flutter?

Flutter stands out from other frameworks due to its ability to create beautiful, high-performance apps with minimal effort. Unlike traditional native development, which requires separate codebases for Android and iOS, Flutter allows developers to use a single codebase to build apps for multiple platforms, including mobile, web, and desktop. This not only saves time and resources but also ensures a consistent and seamless user experience across different devices and operating systems.

Whether you're building a mobile app for a startup, a web app for your business, or even a desktop application for a large enterprise, Flutter enables you to target a broad audience and deliver your product faster than ever before.

What This Book Covers

"Mastering Flutter" provides a thorough exploration of Flutter, starting with foundational concepts and advancing all the way to building complex, production-ready apps. This book is your ultimate guide to understanding how Flutter works, how to leverage its vast library of widgets, and how to integrate essential features like authentication, data storage, animations, and more.

We'll dive into topics such as:

- **Flutter Fundamentals**: From setting up your development environment to building your first app, we cover everything you need to know to get started.
- **Widgets and Layouts**: Understanding Flutter's powerful widget-based architecture, we'll teach you how to create stunning UIs with flexibility, using simple and advanced layout techniques.

- **State Management**: As apps grow more complex, so does managing state. We explore some of the most advanced state management solutions in Flutter, including Provider, Riverpod, BLoC, and Redux.
- **Backend Integration**: Flutter excels at making API calls, handling data, and synchronizing with remote servers. You'll learn how to integrate external APIs, work with Firebase, handle offline data, and manage complex data flows.
- **Animations**: Flutter shines in creating complex, visually appealing animations. This book offers in-depth coverage of how to use **AnimationController**, **Tween**, and **CustomPainter** for building sophisticated animations that bring your app to life.
- **Security and Authentication**: Security is paramount when building apps that deal with sensitive user information. You'll learn how to secure user data, implement robust authentication systems (using JWT, OAuth, and Firebase Authentication), and protect your app from security vulnerabilities.
- **Multi-Platform Development**: We'll cover how Flutter can be used to build **Progressive Web Apps (PWAs)** and desktop applications for macOS, Windows, and Linux, all from a single codebase, making your app truly cross-platform.

- **Testing, Debugging, and Deployment**: This book will walk you through writing tests, debugging your apps, and preparing them for deployment to app stores, ensuring that your apps are robust and production-ready.
- **Continuous Integration and Deployment (CI/CD)**: Learn how to automate the build, test, and deployment processes, streamlining your workflow with CI/CD pipelines.

Why This Book is Essential

As mobile development continues to grow, businesses and developers alike need to embrace cross-platform frameworks like Flutter to meet the demands of an increasingly mobile-first world. By learning Flutter, you gain access to one of the most powerful, flexible, and future-proof tools available. This book not only helps you get started but also provides deep insights into Flutter's advanced features that allow you to scale your apps and build complex systems.

In addition to covering the core aspects of Flutter, **"Mastering Flutter"** offers:

- **Real-World Examples**: We will walk you through building apps like an e-commerce app, a task manager, and a multi-language app, all while covering practical, hands-on examples.

- **Best Practices**: We emphasize best practices for writing clean, maintainable code, structuring large applications, and leveraging Flutter's ecosystem for efficient development.
- **Advanced Topics**: This book includes in-depth chapters on performance optimization, handling animations, integrating third-party services, and managing app state, giving you the tools to tackle even the most complex Flutter projects.

Who This Book is For

This book is for:

- **Beginner Flutter Developers**: If you're new to Flutter, this book starts with the basics and builds up to more advanced concepts. By the end of this book, you'll be able to build fully-featured Flutter apps.
- **Experienced Developers**: If you're already familiar with Flutter, this book covers advanced topics such as state management, animations, backend integration, and multi-platform development, allowing you to take your skills to the next level.
- **Cross-Platform Enthusiasts**: If you're a developer looking to expand your knowledge of building cross-platform apps with Flutter, this book offers practical insights into building for mobile, web, and desktop.

- **App Architects**: Flutter's flexibility makes it a great choice for large-scale applications, and this book will teach you how to scale and structure your apps for performance and maintainability.

Why Learn Flutter?

With Flutter, you can:

- Build beautiful, high-performance apps with ease, even for multiple platforms.
- Streamline your development process and reduce the time spent on creating apps for different platforms.
- Stay ahead of the curve as Flutter continues to evolve and gain popularity in the mobile development community.

Whether you're building your first mobile app or you're a seasoned developer looking to explore Flutter's full potential, **"Mastering Flutter: A Comprehensive Guide to Building Cross-Platform Apps"** equips you with the knowledge and tools you need to succeed.

Conclusion

In this book, we'll guide you step by step through the process of mastering Flutter, from understanding its core concepts to building sophisticated cross-platform apps. By the end, you'll have a deep understanding of Flutter's capabilities, the confidence to build production-ready apps, and the ability to scale your projects for large user bases. Flutter's versatility and power will give you the tools to create apps that stand out and deliver exceptional user experiences.

Let's dive in and begin your journey into mastering Flutter—building beautiful, high-performance apps for any platform has never been easier.

CHAPTER 1

GETTING STARTED WITH FLUTTER

Introduction to Flutter: What It Is and Why It's Powerful

Flutter is an open-source framework developed by Google for building natively compiled applications for mobile, web, and desktop from a single codebase. Its core appeal lies in its ability to allow developers to write a single codebase for both iOS and Android apps, reducing development time and effort. Flutter's power comes from its widget-based architecture, where everything is a widget, enabling developers to have full control over the app's interface and experience. Additionally, Flutter uses Dart, a language also developed by Google, known for its performance and ease of use.

Key reasons Flutter is powerful:

- **Cross-platform development**: Build apps for both iOS and Android without the need for separate codebases.
- **Hot reload**: Allows you to make changes to the code and see the results immediately, speeding up the development process.

- **Performance**: Flutter's native compilation provides excellent performance, ensuring a smooth user experience.
- **Strong community support**: A growing community and rich set of plugins and packages.
- **Customizability**: Full control over every pixel on the screen with its widget-based UI.

In this chapter, we'll go over how to get started with Flutter by installing the necessary tools, setting up the development environment, and writing your first Flutter application.

Installing Flutter and Setting Up Your Development Environment

Before you start writing Flutter applications, you need to install Flutter and set up your development environment. Follow these steps to get Flutter up and running:

1. **Download Flutter SDK**:
   - Go to the official Flutter website: flutter.dev and download the Flutter SDK suitable for your operating system (Windows, macOS, Linux).
   - Extract the archive to an appropriate location on your file system.
2. **Install Dependencies**:

- For **macOS**, you need Xcode (for iOS development) and Android Studio (for Android development).
- For **Windows**, install the latest version of Android Studio and set up the Android SDK.
- For **Linux**, you will need Android Studio and other development tools (e.g., Git, Dart SDK).

3. **Set Up Environment Variables**:
   - For macOS and Linux, add the Flutter SDK to your PATH environment variable.
   - For Windows, follow the instructions in the Flutter setup guide to add Flutter to your system's environment variables.
4. **Install Android Studio**:
   - Download and install Android Studio from developer.android.com.
   - Install the Flutter and Dart plugins within Android Studio for seamless development.
5. **Run Flutter Doctor**:
   - Open a terminal and run the following command to ensure all dependencies are installed correctly:

```
bash
```

```
flutter doctor
```

- Flutter Doctor checks your environment and shows any missing dependencies. It will guide you through resolving them if anything is missing.

By now, your development environment should be set up, and you're ready to start building Flutter apps.

Understanding the Flutter Architecture

To truly harness the power of Flutter, it's essential to understand how the framework is structured and operates. Flutter's architecture is based on a layered approach that provides flexibility and control to developers.

1. **Flutter Engine**:
   - The Flutter Engine is built with C++ and is responsible for rendering the app's UI using Skia (a 2D graphics library). It interfaces with the underlying operating system to render pixels and handle text, images, and animations.
2. **Foundation Layer**:
   - This layer includes the core Flutter framework, providing basic functionality like widgets, animations, and gesture recognition. The

`flutter` package contains essential libraries for these features.

3. **Widgets**:
    - Flutter uses a widget-based system for building UIs. Everything in Flutter is a widget, including text, buttons, and layout structures. Widgets are organized hierarchically, allowing for efficient rendering and customization.
4. **Dart**:
    - Dart is the programming language behind Flutter. It's an object-oriented, class-based language that focuses on performance and simplicity. Dart's Just-In-Time (JIT) and Ahead-Of-Time (AOT) compilation improve the app's performance, especially during development and production.
5. **Platform Channels**:
    - To interact with the native platform (Android or iOS), Flutter uses platform channels. These allow the app to communicate with platform-specific code written in Java (Android) or Swift/Objective-C (iOS), enabling access to features like the camera, location services, etc.

Understanding this architecture helps you grasp how Flutter interacts with the device and why it provides a high level of performance and flexibility.

Writing Your First Flutter Application: "Hello World"

Now that you have Flutter set up, let's create a simple "Hello World" app to see how Flutter works in action.

1. **Create a New Flutter Project**:
    - Open Android Studio (or your preferred IDE).
    - Select "New Flutter Project" and choose a Flutter application.
    - Name your project (e.g., `hello_flutter`), set the location, and ensure Dart is selected as the language.
    - Click "Finish" to generate the project structure.
2. **Edit main.dart**: Open the `lib/main.dart` file. This file contains the main code for your app. By default, Flutter generates a simple app with a counter. Replace it with the following code to display "Hello World":

```
dart

import 'package:flutter/material.dart';

void main() {
  runApp(MyApp());
}
```

```
class MyApp extends StatelessWidget {
  @override
  Widget build(BuildContext context) {
    return MaterialApp(
      home: Scaffold(
        appBar: AppBar(
          title: Text('Hello World App'),
        ),
        body: Center(
          child: Text('Hello, World!'),
        ),
      ),
    );
  }
}
```

3. **Run the App**:
    - To see the app in action, click on the green play button (Run) in Android Studio. This will build and launch your app in an emulator or connected device.
    - You should see a screen with the text “Hello, World!” displayed in the center of the screen.

Running Your First App on iOS and Android Simulators

Now that you've created your app, let's run it on both Android and iOS simulators/emulators.

1. **Running on Android Emulator**:
   - Open Android Studio and create an Android Virtual Device (AVD) if you haven't already.
   - Start the emulator by selecting your AVD and clicking the "Play" button.
   - Once the emulator is running, click on the "Run" button in Android Studio to launch your app on the emulator.
2. **Running on iOS Simulator** (macOS only):
   - Open Xcode and ensure you have an iOS simulator set up.
   - In Android Studio, select the iOS simulator from the available devices.
   - Click on the "Run" button to launch your app on the simulator.

Conclusion

In this chapter, we've set up Flutter, explored its architecture, and created a simple "Hello World" application. You've learned how to run your app on both Android and iOS simulators, marking the first step in your journey toward building powerful cross-platform apps with Flutter. In the next chapter, we'll dive deeper into Dart programming and cover the essential language features that you will use extensively in Flutter development.

CHAPTER 2

DART LANGUAGE BASICS

Introduction to Dart: The Language Behind Flutter

Dart is an object-oriented, class-based programming language developed by Google. It serves as the backbone of Flutter, the cross-platform framework you're using to build mobile, web, and desktop apps. Dart is designed to be easy to learn, efficient in performance, and powerful enough to handle everything from simple scripts to complex applications.

What makes Dart particularly suitable for Flutter development is its asynchronous programming capabilities, which allow developers to manage tasks like network requests, file I/O, and UI updates without blocking the main thread. Dart compiles to native machine code for fast performance, whether you're building for Android, iOS, or the web.

Key features of Dart:

- **JIT (Just-In-Time) Compilation**: Speeds up development by allowing you to test code changes immediately.

- **AOT (Ahead-Of-Time) Compilation**: Compiles the code into optimized, native code for better performance on production apps.
- **Rich Standard Library**: Provides libraries for asynchronous programming, file handling, and more.
- **Null Safety**: Dart ensures that you handle null values properly, improving code reliability.

In this chapter, we'll cover the foundational aspects of the Dart language that you will use frequently when building Flutter apps. From variables to control structures, these basics will form the building blocks for your Flutter applications.

Variables, Data Types, and Control Structures

Let's start with the core building blocks of any programming language: variables, data types, and control structures.

1. **Variables in Dart**: Variables are containers for storing data. In Dart, you can declare a variable using `var`, `final`, or `const` depending on the variable's behavior.
   - **`var`**: Used for variables that can change values.
   - **`final`**: Used for variables that are assigned only once and cannot be reassigned.
   - **`const`**: Used for variables whose value is constant at compile-time.

Example:

```
dart

var name = 'John';     // This can be reassigned
final age = 30;        // This can't be reassigned
const pi = 3.14;     // This is a compile-time constant
```

2. **Data Types in Dart**: Dart supports various data types, including primitive types like integers, floating-point numbers, booleans, and more complex types like objects and collections.
   - **int**: Represents whole numbers.
   - **double**: Represents decimal numbers.
   - **String**: Represents text.
   - **bool**: Represents a boolean value (true or false).
   - **List**: A collection of ordered items (like arrays).
   - **Set**: A collection of unique items.
   - **Map**: A collection of key-value pairs.

Example:

```
dart

int count = 10;
double temperature = 36.6;
```

```
String greeting = 'Hello, Dart!';
bool isActive = true;
List<int> numbers = [1, 2, 3, 4];
```

3. **Control Structures**: Dart offers the usual control structures like loops, conditionals, and switch statements.
    - **If-else Statements**: Used for decision-making.
    - **For Loops**: Used for iterating over a range of values.
    - **While Loops**: Used for repeating a block of code as long as a condition is true.

Example:

```
dart

if (count > 5) {
  print('Count is greater than 5');
} else {
  print('Count is 5 or less');
}

for (var i = 0; i < numbers.length; i++) {
  print(numbers[i]);
}
```

Functions and Methods in Dart

Functions and methods allow you to group code into reusable blocks, making your program more modular and manageable.

1. **Functions**: Functions are defined with the `void` keyword (if they don't return a value) or a specific return type. You can pass data into functions using parameters.

   Example:

   ```
   dart

   // Function without return value
   void greet(String name) {
     print('Hello, $name!');
   }

   // Calling the function
   greet('John');  // Output: Hello, John!

   // Function with return value
   int add(int a, int b) {
     return a + b;
   }

   var sum = add(5, 7);  // sum = 12
   ```

2. **Methods**: Methods are functions that are tied to an object (i.e., a class). They are very similar to functions but are part of a class.

Example:

```
dart

class Person {
  String name;

  Person(this.name);

  void introduce() {
    print('Hi, my name is $name');
  }
}

var person = Person('John');
person.introduce(); // Output: Hi, my name
is John
```

Working with Lists, Sets, and Maps in Dart

Dart provides powerful collection types for managing groups of objects. These include `List`, `Set`, and `Map`.

1. **Lists**: Lists are ordered collections, and you can access elements by their index. Lists in Dart are dynamic, meaning you can add or remove items at any time.

   Example:

```
dart

List<String> fruits = ['Apple', 'Banana',
'Orange'];
fruits.add('Grapes');   // Adds Grapes to
the list
print(fruits[1]);  // Output: Banana
```

2. **Sets**: Sets are unordered collections that store unique values. They automatically remove duplicates.

   Example:

```
dart

Set<int> numbers = {1, 2, 3, 4};
numbers.add(3);  // Duplicate value, won't
be added
print(numbers);  // Output: {1, 2, 3, 4}
```

3. **Maps**: Maps are collections of key-value pairs, where each key is unique. You can access values using their corresponding keys.

   Example:

```
dart

Map<String, String> capitals = {
  'USA': 'Washington, D.C.',
```

```
    'UK': 'London',
    'India': 'New Delhi'
  };
  print(capitals['UK']);  // Output: London
```

Real-World Example: Building a Simple Dart Program

Let's build a simple Dart program that asks the user for their name and age, and then displays a greeting message based on their input.

```
dart

import 'dart:io';

void main() {
  print('Enter your name:');
  String? name = stdin.readLineSync();

  print('Enter your age:');
  int age = int.parse(stdin.readLineSync()!);

  print('Hello, $name! You are $age years old.');
}
```

In this program:

- The user is prompted to input their name and age using the `stdin.readLineSync()` method.

- The `int.parse()` method is used to convert the user's input into an integer.
- Finally, the program displays a greeting message using the `print()` function.

Conclusion

In this chapter, we covered the basics of Dart, including variables, data types, control structures, functions, and methods. We also explored how to work with collections like lists, sets, and maps. With these fundamentals, you now have the essential tools needed to start building more complex Flutter applications. In the next chapter, we'll dive into Flutter's widget-based architecture and begin designing our first UI.

CHAPTER 3

FLUTTER WIDGETS: THE BUILDING BLOCKS

What Are Flutter Widgets?

In Flutter, everything is a widget. This includes visual elements like buttons, text, and images, as well as structural elements like rows, columns, and grids. A widget is a basic building block of your Flutter application's UI, and it is the key concept that makes Flutter's user interface declarative and flexible.

Widgets are used to describe the user interface, and they determine how the app looks and responds to user interaction. Flutter's widget system is hierarchical, meaning widgets can be composed of other widgets to create complex interfaces. Each widget has a corresponding configuration, a state (if needed), and a rendering mechanism.

Widgets can be broadly divided into two categories:

- **Visual Widgets**: These represent things you see on the screen, such as `Text`, `Icon`, `Container`, and `Image`.

- **Structural Widgets**: These define the layout structure and how visual widgets are arranged, such as `Row`, `Column`, and `Stack`.

Stateless vs. Stateful Widgets

Flutter divides widgets into two types based on whether or not they maintain any mutable state: **Stateless Widgets** and **Stateful Widgets**.

1. **Stateless Widgets**:
    - A stateless widget is immutable, meaning it doesn't change after it is built. These widgets do not hold any mutable state and are simply used to display static information.
    - Stateless widgets are often used when the UI does not depend on user interaction or data that changes over time.

    Example:

    ```
    dart

    class MyHomePage extends StatelessWidget {
      @override
      Widget build(BuildContext context) {
    ```

```
    return Scaffold(
      appBar: AppBar(title: Text("Welcome to Flutter")),
      body: Center(child: Text("Hello, World!")),
    );
  }
}
```

In this example, `MyHomePage` is a stateless widget that only displays a static text string and doesn't change during the app's lifecycle.

2. **Stateful Widgets**:
    - A stateful widget is mutable, meaning it can rebuild itself whenever its internal state changes. This is ideal when the UI needs to update in response to user interaction or other dynamic changes.
    - Stateful widgets contain a state object that is responsible for holding the widget's mutable state.

Example:

```
dart

class CounterPage extends StatefulWidget {
  @override
```

```
  _CounterPageState    createState()    =>
_CounterPageState();
}

class      _CounterPageState      extends
State<CounterPage> {
  int _counter = 0;

  void _incrementCounter() {
    setState(() {
      _counter++;
    });
  }

  @override
  Widget build(BuildContext context) {
    return Scaffold(
      appBar: AppBar(title: Text("Counter
App")),
      body: Center(
        child: Column(
          mainAxisAlignment:
MainAxisAlignment.center,
          children: <Widget>[
            Text('Counter: $_counter'),
            ElevatedButton(
              onPressed:
_incrementCounter,
              child: Text('Increment'),
```

```
              ),
            ],
          ),
        ),
      );
    }
  }
```

In this example, `CounterPage` is a stateful widget that updates the `_counter` variable whenever the user presses the "Increment" button, causing the UI to refresh with the new counter value.

Basic Widgets: Text, Container, Column, Row

Now, let's explore some of the most commonly used Flutter widgets to build the foundation of your UI.

1. **Text**:
   - The `Text` widget is used to display text on the screen. You can customize its appearance with various properties such as `style`, `textAlign`, and `overflow`.

   Example:

   `dart`

```
Text(
  'Hello, Flutter!',
  style: TextStyle(fontSize: 24, color:
Colors.blue),
)
```

2. **Container**:
    - The `Container` widget is one of the most versatile widgets in Flutter. It allows you to add padding, margins, decoration (like colors, borders, and shadows), and constraints (such as width and height).

Example:

```
dart

Container(
  width: 200,
  height: 100,
  decoration: BoxDecoration(
    color: Colors.green,
    borderRadius:
BorderRadius.circular(10),
  ),
  child: Center(child: Text('Styled
Container')),
)
```

3. **Column**:
   - The `Column` widget arranges its children vertically. You can control how the children are aligned using properties like `mainAxisAlignment` and `crossAxisAlignment`.

Example:

```
dart

Column(
  mainAxisAlignment:
MainAxisAlignment.center,
  children: <Widget>[
    Text('First Item'),
    Text('Second Item'),
    Text('Third Item'),
  ],
)
```

4. **Row**:
   - The `Row` widget arranges its children horizontally. Similar to `Column`, you can control alignment and spacing between the elements inside a row.

Example:

```
dart

Row(
  mainAxisAlignment:
MainAxisAlignment.spaceEvenly,
  children: <Widget>[
    Icon(Icons.home),
    Icon(Icons.favorite),
    Icon(Icons.settings),
  ],
)
```

Using Common Layout Widgets: Stack, ListView, GridView

As you begin building more complex UIs, you will frequently use layout widgets that help organize your app's elements.

1. **Stack**:
    - A `Stack` allows you to layer widgets on top of each other. The first widget is drawn at the bottom, and subsequent widgets are drawn above it.

    Example:

    ```
    dart

    Stack(
    ```

```
  children: <Widget>[
    Container(
      width: 200,
      height: 200,
      color: Colors.blue,
    ),
    Positioned(
      top: 50,
      left: 50,
      child: Container(
        width: 100,
        height: 100,
        color: Colors.red,
      ),
    ),
  ],
)
```

In this example, a red `Container` is placed on top of a blue `Container`, and the red container is positioned using the `Positioned` widget.

2. **ListView**:
   - `ListView` is a scrollable list of widgets, ideal for displaying large datasets or long lists of items.

Example:

```
dart
```

```
ListView(
  children: <Widget>[
    ListTile(
      leading: Icon(Icons.access_alarm),
      title: Text('Item 1'),
    ),
    ListTile(
      leading: Icon(Icons.accessibility),
      title: Text('Item 2'),
    ),
  ],
)
```

3. **GridView**:
   - `GridView` is a scrollable 2D array of widgets. It's perfect for displaying items in a grid, like image galleries or product lists.

Example:

```
dart

GridView.count(
  crossAxisCount: 2,
  children: <Widget>[
    Container(color: Colors.blue, child:
Center(child: Text('Item 1'))),
```

```
    Container(color: Colors.green, child:
Center(child: Text('Item 2'))),
    Container(color: Colors.red, child:
Center(child: Text('Item 3'))),
  ],
)
```

In this example, `GridView.count` creates a grid with 2 columns, and each container represents an individual grid item.

Real-World Example: Creating a Simple UI with Multiple Widgets

Let's combine several widgets to build a simple Flutter app UI. The app will display a greeting message, a list of items, and a button that can be clicked to increment a counter.

```
dart

import 'package:flutter/material.dart';

void main() => runApp(MyApp());

class MyApp extends StatefulWidget {
  @override
  _MyAppState createState() => _MyAppState();
```

```
}

class _MyAppState extends State<MyApp> {
  int _counter = 0;

  void _incrementCounter() {
    setState(() {
      _counter++;
    });
  }

  @override
  Widget build(BuildContext context) {
    return MaterialApp(
      home: Scaffold(
        appBar: AppBar(
          title: Text('Simple UI with Multiple
Widgets'),
        ),
        body: Padding(
          padding: const EdgeInsets.all(16.0),
          child: Column(
            mainAxisAlignment:
MainAxisAlignment.center,
            children: <Widget>[
              Text(
                'Hello, Flutter!',
                style: TextStyle(fontSize: 24,
fontWeight: FontWeight.bold),
```

```
              ),
              SizedBox(height: 20),
              Text('Counter: $_counter', style:
TextStyle(fontSize: 20)),
              ElevatedButton(
                onPressed: _incrementCounter,
                child:           Text('Increment
Counter'),
              ),
              SizedBox(height: 20),
              ListView(
                shrinkWrap: true,
                children: <Widget>[
                  ListTile(title:     Text('Item
1')),
                  ListTile(title:     Text('Item
2')),
                  ListTile(title:     Text('Item
3')),
                ],
              ),
            ],
          ),
        ),
      ),
    );
  }
}
```

In this real-world example:

- We use a `Column` to arrange a greeting message, a counter display, a button, and a `ListView` in the same layout.
- The `ElevatedButton` increments the `_counter` when clicked, demonstrating state changes with a `StatefulWidget`.
- The `ListView` displays a list of items below the button.

Conclusion

In this chapter, you've learned about Flutter's widget-based architecture and how to build UIs with common Flutter widgets like `Text`, `Container`, `Column`, `Row`, `Stack`, `ListView`, and `GridView`. These widgets form the building blocks for your Flutter applications. You also learned the difference between `StatelessWidget` and `StatefulWidget`, and how to manage state changes in your app. In the next chapter, we'll dive into how to make your app interactive by handling user input and managing form data.

CHAPTER 4

BUILDING LAYOUTS WITH FLUTTER

Understanding Flutter's Layout System

Flutter uses a flexible and responsive layout system based on **widgets**. At its core, the layout system is based on the `widget tree`, which organizes the UI components hierarchically. Each widget defines how the layout behaves in a given space.

There are two key types of layout widgets in Flutter:

1. **Flex-based Layouts**: These are widgets like `Row`, `Column`, `Flex`, and `Expanded`, which allow you to organize and align widgets in either a horizontal (row) or vertical (column) direction. These layout types are more flexible and are widely used in creating responsive UIs.
2. **Positioned-based Layouts**: These layouts are used when you need to control where a widget is placed on the screen, for example, using `Stack` and `Positioned`.

Flutter's layout system works by passing size constraints from parent widgets to child widgets. The child widget then decides how much space to take up based on the constraints. This system provides a high degree of flexibility and performance optimization.

Building Responsive Layouts with Flex and Expanded

In Flutter, creating flexible and responsive layouts often involves using `Row`, `Column`, `Flex`, and `Expanded`. These widgets allow you to distribute space dynamically within a parent widget.

1. **Row**:
   - A `Row` widget is used to arrange child widgets horizontally. The width of the children is determined by their content size unless you use layout widgets like `Expanded`.

   Example:

   ```
   dart

   Row(
     children: <Widget>[
       Icon(Icons.home),
       Icon(Icons.favorite),
       Icon(Icons.settings),
     ],
   )
   ```

This creates a simple horizontal row of icons. You can add flexibility by wrapping individual items with `Expanded` or `Flexible`.

2. **Column**:
   - Similar to `Row`, a `Column` widget arranges child widgets vertically.

Example:

```
dart

Column(
  children: <Widget>[
    Text('Item 1'),
    Text('Item 2'),
    Text('Item 3'),
  ],
)
```

3. **Flex**:
   - The `Flex` widget allows you to arrange children either horizontally or vertically based on its `direction` property. It is like `Row` or `Column`, but more customizable.

Example:

```
dart
```

```
Flex(
  direction: Axis.horizontal,
  children: <Widget>[
    Text('Item 1'),
    Text('Item 2'),
    Text('Item 3'),
  ],
)
```

4. **Expanded**:
   - The `Expanded` widget helps divide available space among the children of a `Row` or `Column` evenly. It forces its child widget to take up the remaining space in the parent widget.

Example:

dart

```
Row(
  children: <Widget>[
    Icon(Icons.home),
    Expanded(child: Text('Center')),
    Icon(Icons.settings),
  ],
)
```

Here, the `Text` widget will take up the remaining horizontal space in the row, ensuring that the icons have only the space they need.

5. **Flexible**:
   - `Flexible` works similarly to `Expanded`, but with more control over how the available space is divided. You can use the `flex` property to control the proportion of space each child takes.

Example:

```
dart

Row(
  children: <Widget>[
    Flexible(flex: 1, child:
Icon(Icons.home)),
    Flexible(flex: 2, child:
Icon(Icons.favorite)),
  ],
)
```

In this example, the `Icon` with `Icons.favorite` will take up twice the space of the `Icon` with `Icons.home`.

Aligning Widgets Using Alignment and Padding

In Flutter, alignment and padding are crucial for controlling the positioning and spacing of widgets. You can use these widgets to adjust how content appears on the screen and ensure a responsive and well-structured layout.

1. **Alignment**:
   - The `Align` widget allows you to position a child widget within its parent widget. You can use the `alignment` property to position the widget along the x and y axes.

   Example:

   ```
   dart

   Align(
     alignment: Alignment.topLeft,
     child: Text('Top Left'),
   )
   ```

   In this example, the `Text` widget is aligned to the top-left of the parent.

2. **Padding**:
   - The `Padding` widget adds space around its child widget. It's commonly used to create spacing between elements and to prevent them from touching the edges of the screen or other widgets.

Example:

```
dart

Padding(
  padding: EdgeInsets.all(16.0),
  child: Text('This text has padding'),
)
```

Here, `EdgeInsets.all(16.0)` adds 16 pixels of padding on all sides of the `Text` widget.

3. **Container (for alignment and padding)**:
   - The `Container` widget can also be used for both alignment and padding. It is highly versatile and allows you to apply multiple properties, such as padding, margin, and alignment.

Example:

```
dart

Container(
  padding: EdgeInsets.all(20),
  alignment: Alignment.center,
  color: Colors.blue,
  child:    Text('Centered    text    with
padding'),
)
```

Using the Scaffold Widget for Basic App Structure

The `Scaffold` widget provides a basic app structure and is one of the most important widgets in Flutter. It includes slots for common visual elements, such as the app bar, drawer, body, bottom navigation, and floating action buttons. The `Scaffold` ensures consistency in your app's layout.

Here are the key properties of a `Scaffold`:

- **AppBar**: A top bar with the title or action buttons.
- **Body**: The main content of your app.
- **Drawer**: A slide-out menu, often used for navigation.
- **BottomNavigationBar**: A bar at the bottom for navigating between screens.
- **FloatingActionButton**: A floating action button that typically triggers a primary action.

Example:

```
dart

Scaffold(
  appBar: AppBar(
    title: Text('Flutter Layout Example'),
  ),
  body: Center(
```

```
    child: Text('Hello, Flutter!'),
  ),
  floatingActionButton: FloatingActionButton(
    onPressed: () {
      // Define your action here
    },
    child: Icon(Icons.add),
  ),
)
```

In this example:

- The `Scaffold` contains an `AppBar` with a title.
- The body of the app contains a centered `Text` widget.
- A `FloatingActionButton` is positioned in the bottom-right corner.

Real-World Example: Creating a Flexible App Layout

Let’s create a simple app that demonstrates a flexible layout. This app will contain a header, a list of items, and a footer. The layout will adjust based on the screen size.

```
dart

import 'package:flutter/material.dart';
```

```
void main() => runApp(MyApp());

class MyApp extends StatelessWidget {
  @override
  Widget build(BuildContext context) {
    return MaterialApp(
      home: Scaffold(
        appBar: AppBar(title: Text('Flexible
Layout Example')),
        body: Column(
          children: <Widget>[
            Container(
              padding: EdgeInsets.all(20),
              alignment: Alignment.center,
              color: Colors.blue,
              child: Text(
                'Header Section',
                style: TextStyle(color:
Colors.white, fontSize: 24),
              ),
            ),
            Expanded(
              child: ListView(
                children: <Widget>[
                  ListTile(title: Text('Item
1')),
                  ListTile(title: Text('Item
2')),
```

```
                  ListTile(title:     Text('Item
3')),
                  ListTile(title:     Text('Item
4')),
                  ListTile(title:     Text('Item
5')),
                ],
              ),
            ),
            Container(
              padding: EdgeInsets.all(20),
              alignment: Alignment.center,
              color: Colors.blue,
              child: Text(
                'Footer Section',
                style:          TextStyle(color:
Colors.white, fontSize: 24),
              ),
            ),
          ],
        ),
      ),
    );
  }
}
```

In this app:

- The `Column` widget arranges the header, body, and footer vertically.
- The header and footer are `Container` widgets with a blue background and centered text.
- The body is an `Expanded` widget that contains a `ListView` with several list items. The `Expanded` widget allows the `ListView` to take up the remaining space, making the layout flexible.

This example demonstrates a simple, responsive layout using the `Column`, `Container`, `Expanded`, and `ListView` widgets. The layout will adjust depending on the screen size, making it suitable for different devices.

Conclusion

In this chapter, you learned how to build layouts in Flutter using widgets like `Row`, `Column`, `Flex`, `Expanded`, `Padding`, and `Align`. You also explored how the `Scaffold` widget provides the basic structure for your app's interface, including app bars, floating action buttons, and more. We demonstrated a real-world example of a flexible layout using these widgets. In the next chapter, we will dive into handling user input and forms to make your app interactive.

CHAPTER 5

FLUTTER NAVIGATION AND ROUTING

Managing App Screens with Navigation

In Flutter, navigation is the process of managing the transition between different screens (or "pages") of your app. Proper navigation is crucial for building multi-screen apps and providing a seamless user experience. Flutter's navigation system is based on the **Navigator** widget, which is used to manage a stack of screens.

The `Navigator` widget works similarly to a stack of cards. Each time you navigate to a new screen, the current screen is pushed onto the stack. When you navigate back, the current screen is popped off the stack, returning to the previous screen.

Key Concepts in Navigation:

- **Pushing a screen**: Moving from one screen to another.
- **Popping a screen**: Going back to the previous screen.
- **Routing**: Mapping screens to their corresponding paths or routes.

To manage navigation in Flutter, you primarily work with the `Navigator` class, which handles the stack of screens and the transitions between them.

Using Navigator to Switch Between Screens

To navigate between screens, you can use the `Navigator.push()` and `Navigator.pop()` methods. `push()` adds a new screen to the stack, while `pop()` removes the current screen, returning to the previous one.

Pushing a Screen (Navigating Forward):

To navigate to a new screen, you use `Navigator.push()`. This requires the `context` and the screen you want to navigate to.

Example:

```
dart

Navigator.push(
  context,
  MaterialPageRoute(builder:     (context)     =>
SecondScreen()),
);
```

In this example:

- `MaterialPageRoute` is used to define the route for the `SecondScreen`.
- The `context` is passed to `Navigator.push()` to maintain the correct navigation context.

Popping a Screen (Navigating Back):

To navigate back to the previous screen, you use `Navigator.pop()`.

Example:

```
dart

Navigator.pop(context);
```

This will remove the current screen from the stack and return to the previous one.

Passing Data Between Screens

When navigating between screens, it's often necessary to pass data to the destination screen. In Flutter, you can pass data via the constructor of the screen you are navigating to, or you can use named routes with arguments.

Passing Data through Constructors:

When you create the screen, you can pass data through the constructor.

Example:

```dart
Navigator.push(
  context,
  MaterialPageRoute(
    builder: (context) => SecondScreen(data: 'Hello from the first screen'),
  ),
);
```

In the `SecondScreen` widget:

```dart
class SecondScreen extends StatelessWidget {
  final String data;

  SecondScreen({required this.data});

  @override
  Widget build(BuildContext context) {
    return Scaffold(
      appBar: AppBar(title: Text('Second Screen')),
      body: Center(child: Text(data)),
```

```
    );
  }
}
```

In this example, the `SecondScreen` receives the data passed through its constructor and displays it on the screen.

Named Routes and Route Management

Named routes provide a more structured way to navigate between screens. They allow you to define routes in a central place, typically in your `MaterialApp` widget, and then navigate using route names instead of passing entire widget objects.

Defining Named Routes:

In Flutter, you define named routes in the `MaterialApp` widget by providing a `routes` map that associates route names with screen widgets.

Example:

```
dart

MaterialApp(
  initialRoute: '/',
  routes: {
```

```
      '/': (context) => FirstScreen(),
      '/second': (context) => SecondScreen(),
   },
);
```

Here, we have two named routes:

- `'/'`: The home screen (FirstScreen).
- `'/second'`: The second screen (SecondScreen).

Navigating with Named Routes:

To navigate to a named route, you use `Navigator.pushNamed()` and provide the name of the route.

Example:

```
dart

Navigator.pushNamed(context, '/second');
```

This will navigate to the screen associated with the `/second` route, which is the `SecondScreen`.

Passing Arguments with Named Routes:

You can pass arguments to named routes using the `arguments` property of `Navigator.pushNamed()`.

Example:

```dart
Navigator.pushNamed(
  context,
  '/second',
  arguments: 'Hello from the first screen',
);
```

In the destination screen, you can retrieve the arguments using the `ModalRoute.of(context)?.settings.arguments`.

```dart
class SecondScreen extends StatelessWidget {
  @override
  Widget build(BuildContext context) {
    final String data = ModalRoute.of(context)?.settings.arguments as String;
    return Scaffold(
      appBar: AppBar(title: Text('Second Screen')),
      body: Center(child: Text(data)),
    );
  }
}
```

Real-World Example: Building a Multi-Screen App with Navigation

Let's build a simple Flutter app with two screens. The first screen will contain a button that navigates to the second screen, passing some data. The second screen will display the data.

Step 1: Defining the Screens

```
dart

import 'package:flutter/material.dart';

void main() => runApp(MyApp());

class MyApp extends StatelessWidget {
  @override
  Widget build(BuildContext context) {
    return MaterialApp(
      initialRoute: '/',
      routes: {
        '/': (context) => FirstScreen(),
        '/second': (context) => SecondScreen(),
      },
    );
  }
}

class FirstScreen extends StatelessWidget {
```

```
  @override
  Widget build(BuildContext context) {
    return Scaffold(
      appBar:     AppBar(title:     Text('First
Screen')),
      body: Center(
        child: ElevatedButton(
          onPressed: () {
            // Navigate to the second screen with
data
            Navigator.pushNamed(
              context,
              '/second',
              arguments: 'Hello from the first
screen!',
            );
          },
          child: Text('Go to Second Screen'),
        ),
      ),
    );
  }
}

class SecondScreen extends StatelessWidget {
  @override
  Widget build(BuildContext context) {
    // Retrieve the arguments passed to the
second screen
```

```
    final String data = ModalRoute.of(context)?.settings.arguments as String;

    return Scaffold(
      appBar: AppBar(title: Text('Second Screen')),
      body: Center(
        child: Text(data),
      ),
    );
  }
}
```

Step 2: Navigating Between Screens

- When the user presses the button on the `FirstScreen`, they are navigated to the `SecondScreen`.
- The data, `"Hello from the first screen!"`, is passed to the second screen via the `arguments` property of `Navigator.pushNamed()`.

Step 3: Retrieving Data in the Second Screen

- On the `SecondScreen`, we use `ModalRoute.of(context)?.settings.arguments` to retrieve the data passed from the first screen and display it in a `Text` widget.

Conclusion

In this chapter, we explored Flutter's navigation and routing system. We learned how to manage screens using the `Navigator` widget, pass data between screens, and implement named routes for cleaner and more organized routing. Additionally, we built a simple real-world example that demonstrates navigation and data passing between multiple screens. In the next chapter, we will focus on handling user input and forms to make your app interactive.

CHAPTER 6

WORKING WITH USER INPUT

Text Input and Form Validation

In Flutter, handling user input is essential for creating interactive apps. Flutter provides various widgets to collect text input from users, such as the `TextField` and `TextFormField`. These widgets are highly customizable and can be used to create forms that collect user data and validate it before submission.

1. **TextField**:
   - The `TextField` widget is the most commonly used widget for accepting text input from users. You can specify the type of text (e.g., password, email, etc.) and manage the input behavior.

Example:

```
dart

TextField(
  decoration: InputDecoration(
    labelText: 'Enter your name',
  ),
```

```
  onChanged: (text) {
    print('User typed: $text');
  },
);
```

This code creates a `TextField` with a label asking for the user's name. The `onChanged` callback prints the text typed by the user.

2. **TextFormField**:
   - `TextFormField` is an enhanced version of `TextField` that integrates seamlessly with form validation. It works well in conjunction with the `Form` widget, which helps group multiple form fields and manage their validation and submission.

Example:

```
dart

final _formKey = GlobalKey<FormState>();

TextFormField(
  decoration: InputDecoration(
    labelText: 'Email',
    hintText: 'Enter your email',
  ),
  validator: (value) {
```

```
        if (value == null || value.isEmpty) {
          return 'Please enter some text';
        }
        return null;
      },
    );
```

The `validator` function checks if the input is empty and returns an error message if it is. You can add more complex validation logic as needed.

3. **Form Validation**:
   - To validate a form, wrap the form fields inside a `Form` widget and use the `GlobalKey<FormState>` to manage the form's state.

Example:

```
dart

Form(
  key: _formKey,
  child: Column(
    children: <Widget>[
      TextFormField(
        validator: (value) {
          if (value == null ||
value.isEmpty) {
```

```
            return 'Please enter your
email';
          }
          return null;
        },
      ),
      ElevatedButton(
        onPressed: () {
          if
(_formKey.currentState?.validate() ??
false) {
            // If the form is valid,
proceed with form submission
          } else {
            // Handle invalid form
          }
        },
        child: Text('Submit'),
      ),
    ],
  ),
);
```

In this example, when the user presses the submit button, the `validate()` method is called, and if the form is valid, further actions (like form submission) can occur.

Handling Buttons, Sliders, and Switches

1. **Buttons**:
   - Flutter offers several types of buttons, such as `ElevatedButton`, `TextButton`, and `IconButton`, to handle user interactions.

Example:

```dart
ElevatedButton(
  onPressed: () {
    // Perform some action
    print('Button Pressed!');
  },
  child: Text('Click Me'),
);
```

`onPressed` is the callback that gets triggered when the button is tapped. You can define any action inside it, such as navigation or submitting form data.

2. **Sliders**:
   - A `Slider` widget allows the user to select a value from a range. It can be used to get a numerical input, such as a rating or volume control.

Example:

```dart
Slider(
  value: _sliderValue,
  min: 0,
  max: 100,
  onChanged: (value) {
    setState(() {
      _sliderValue = value;
    });
  },
);
```

The value of `_sliderValue` changes as the slider is moved, and the widget updates accordingly with the `setState()` method.

3. **Switches**:
   - A `Switch` widget is used for binary choices, such as turning a setting on or off.

Example:

```dart
Switch(
  value: _isSwitched,
  onChanged: (value) {
    setState(() {
```

```
        _isSwitched = value;
      });
    },
  );
```

When the user toggles the switch, the state is updated using `setState()`, and the widget is rebuilt to reflect the new state.

Gesture Detection for Touch Events

Flutter allows you to detect various gestures, such as taps, swipes, and drags, using the `GestureDetector` widget. This widget can detect gestures on any child widget, enabling interactive elements like buttons or custom controls.

1. **GestureDetector**:
   - The `GestureDetector` widget listens for gestures and triggers the corresponding callback.

   Example:

   dart

```
GestureDetector(
  onTap: () {
    print('Tapped on the screen!');
```

```
    },
    onLongPress: () {
      print('Long pressed on the screen!');
    },
    child: Container(
      width: 100,
      height: 100,
      color: Colors.blue,
    ),
  );
```

In this example, the `GestureDetector` detects both tap and long press gestures and prints a message to the console when the user performs either gesture on the `Container` widget.

2. **Other Gestures**:
    - Flutter supports several other gestures like `onPanUpdate`, `onVerticalDragUpdate`, and `onHorizontalDragUpdate` for detecting drag movements. These gestures can be used for more interactive components like sliders or drag-and-drop functionality.

Handling Keyboard Events and Focus

Handling keyboard events and managing focus are key aspects of working with forms and text input fields. Flutter provides the `FocusNode` class and `TextInput` API to manage focus and interact with the keyboard.

1. **FocusNode**:
    - A `FocusNode` is used to manage the focus state of a widget. You can use it to listen for focus changes or request focus on a specific widget.

Example:

```
dart

FocusNode _focusNode = FocusNode();

TextField(
  focusNode: _focusNode,
  decoration: InputDecoration(labelText:
'Username'),
);
```

In this example, the `FocusNode` is assigned to the `TextField`. You can control whether the text field is focused and trigger actions when the field gains or loses focus.

2. **Keyboard Visibility**:

- You can also use the `FocusNode` to detect whether the keyboard is visible and handle UI changes accordingly.

Example:

```
dart

_focusNode.addListener(() {
  if (_focusNode.hasFocus) {
    print('Keyboard is visible');
  } else {
    print('Keyboard is hidden');
  }
});
```

This listens for changes in focus and prints whether the keyboard is visible based on whether the `TextField` is focused.

Real-World Example: Building a Simple Login Form

Let's apply what we've learned and build a simple login form with text input, form validation, and a button to submit the form.

```
dart
```

```
import 'package:flutter/material.dart';

void main() {
  runApp(MyApp());
}

class MyApp extends StatelessWidget {
  @override
  Widget build(BuildContext context) {
    return MaterialApp(
      home: LoginScreen(),
    );
  }
}

class LoginScreen extends StatefulWidget {
  @override
  _LoginScreenState          createState()          =>
_LoginScreenState();
}

class           _LoginScreenState            extends
State<LoginScreen> {
  final _formKey = GlobalKey<FormState>();
  String _username = '';
  String _password = '';

  void _submitForm() {
```

```
    if    (_formKey.currentState?.validate()    ??
false) {

ScaffoldMessenger.of(context).showSnackBar(Snac
kBar(content: Text('Logging in...')));
      // Perform login logic here
    }
  }

  @override
  Widget build(BuildContext context) {
    return Scaffold(
      appBar: AppBar(title: Text('Login')),
      body: Padding(
        padding: const EdgeInsets.all(16.0),
        child: Form(
          key: _formKey,
          child: Column(
            crossAxisAlignment:
CrossAxisAlignment.start,
            children: <Widget>[
              TextFormField(
                decoration:
InputDecoration(labelText: 'Username'),
                validator: (value) {
                  if    (value    ==    null    ||
value.isEmpty) {
                    return   'Please   enter   your
username';
```

```
                }
                return null;
              },
              onChanged:        (value)        =>
setState(() => _username = value),
            ),
            TextFormField(
              obscureText: true,
              decoration:
InputDecoration(labelText: 'Password'),
              validator: (value) {
                if    (value    ==    null    ||
value.isEmpty) {
                  return  'Please  enter  your
password';
                }
                return null;
              },
              onChanged:        (value)        =>
setState(() => _password = value),
            ),
            SizedBox(height: 20),
            ElevatedButton(
              onPressed: _submitForm,
              child: Text('Login'),
            ),
          ],
        ),
      ),
```

```
        ),
      );
    }
}
```

In this example:

- We use a `Form` widget to group the input fields and handle validation.
- The `TextFormField` widgets are used to accept the username and password, with validation to ensure that they are not empty.
- The `ElevatedButton` triggers the form submission, and the app shows a `SnackBar` with a message once the form is validated.

Conclusion

In this chapter, you learned how to work with user input in Flutter. We covered how to handle text input, validate forms, and manage various interactive elements like buttons, sliders, and switches. We also explored gesture detection and handling keyboard events with focus management. Finally, we built a simple login form as a real-world example of how to implement these concepts together. In the next chapter, we'll dive into Flutter's layout system to build more complex and responsive UIs.

CHAPTER 7

STYLING YOUR APP

Introduction to Flutter's Styling System

Flutter provides a powerful and flexible styling system that allows developers to create visually appealing apps. The styling system in Flutter is based on **widgets**, and you can customize almost every aspect of the UI by modifying the properties of these widgets.

Key aspects of Flutter's styling system include:

- **Themes**: Global styling that can be applied throughout the app.
- **Custom Widgets**: Ability to modify individual widgets with properties like colors, padding, fonts, and more.
- **Material Design**: A consistent design language that Flutter supports out-of-the-box for building modern, responsive UIs.

Flutter uses a **declarative** style of UI design, meaning you define the UI using widgets and their properties, and Flutter takes care of rendering the visual output.

Using Themes for Global Styling

Themes in Flutter allow you to define global style settings for your app. By using themes, you can ensure that your app's appearance is consistent across all screens and widgets. You can define the colors, typography, and other visual elements globally, which simplifies maintaining a consistent style.

1. **Defining a Theme**: To apply a theme globally across your app, you use the `ThemeData` class within the `MaterialApp` widget. The `theme` property of `MaterialApp` allows you to set the colors, text styles, and more.

   Example:

   ```
   dart

   MaterialApp(
     theme: ThemeData(
       primarySwatch:   Colors.blue,        //
   Primary color of the app
       accentColor: Colors.orange,  // Accent
   color used for floating action buttons,
   etc.
       textTheme: TextTheme(
   ```

```
      bodyText1:  TextStyle(fontSize:  18,
fontWeight: FontWeight.normal),
      bodyText2:  TextStyle(fontSize:  16,
fontWeight: FontWeight.normal),
      headline1:  TextStyle(fontSize:  32,
fontWeight: FontWeight.bold),
    ),
  ),
  home: MyHomePage(),
);
```

In this example:

- The `primarySwatch` sets the primary color for the app.
- The `accentColor` is used for secondary UI elements, such as floating action buttons.
- The `textTheme` defines global text styles that are applied throughout the app.

2. **Using Theme in Widgets**: Once a theme is defined, you can use it within widgets. For example, to use the theme's primary color in a widget, you can access it through the `Theme.of(context)` method.

   Example:

```
dart

Container(
```

```
  color:   Theme.of(context).primaryColor,
// Accessing the primary color from the
theme
  child: Text(
    'Hello, Flutter!',
    style:
Theme.of(context).textTheme.headline1,  //
Accessing headline1 text style from the
theme
  ),
);
```

By using themes, you ensure that all your widgets automatically adapt to the global styling defined in `MaterialApp`.

Customizing Widgets with Colors, Fonts, and Borders

Flutter allows extensive customization of widgets by adjusting properties like colors, fonts, borders, and padding. This flexibility helps you create visually appealing and user-friendly interfaces.

1. **Color**:
   - You can customize the color of most widgets using the `color` property or the `decoration` property for more complex styling (e.g., `Container`).

Example:

```
dart

Container(
  color: Colors.blue,  // Background color
  child: Text(
    'Styled Text',
    style: TextStyle(color: Colors.white),
// Text color
  ),
);
```

2. **Fonts**:
   - You can set custom fonts by modifying the `TextStyle` widget. You can also use system fonts or import custom fonts.

Example:

```
dart

Text(
  'Custom Font Text',
  style: TextStyle(
    fontFamily: 'Roboto',  // Using a
custom font family
    fontSize: 20,
    fontWeight: FontWeight.bold,
```

```
  ),
);
```

To use custom fonts in your Flutter app, add the font files to the `assets` folder and update your `pubspec.yaml` file.

3. **Borders**:
    - The `BoxDecoration` widget is used to apply borders, shadows, and other decoration properties to containers.

Example:

```
dart

Container(
  decoration: BoxDecoration(
    border: Border.all(color: Colors.blue,
width: 2),
    borderRadius:
BorderRadius.circular(10),
  ),
  child: Text('Bordered Text'),
);
```

This adds a blue border around the container and rounds the corners with a radius of 10 pixels.

4. **Padding and Margin**:
   - You can adjust the padding and margin around widgets using the `Padding` and `Container` widgets respectively.

Example:

```
dart

Padding(
  padding:   EdgeInsets.all(16.0),       //
Padding around the widget
  child: Text('Padded Text'),
);
```

Here, the `EdgeInsets.all(16.0)` adds 16 pixels of padding on all sides of the text widget.

Creating Consistent UI with Material Design

Flutter comes with built-in support for Material Design, a design language developed by Google. Material Design provides a set of guidelines and components that help create visually appealing and consistent UIs. Flutter includes a set of widgets that follow these guidelines, ensuring that your app looks modern and consistent.

Material Widgets:

1. **AppBar**:
   - The `AppBar` widget is used to display the app's title and provide actions like search or navigation buttons.

Example:

```
dart

AppBar(
  title: Text('Material AppBar'),
  actions: [
    IconButton(
      icon: Icon(Icons.search),
      onPressed: () {},
    ),
  ],
)
```

2. **FloatingActionButton**:
   - A floating action button (FAB) is a circular button that hovers above the UI and performs an important action.

Example:

```
dart

FloatingActionButton(
```

```
    onPressed: () {},
    child: Icon(Icons.add),
  )
```

3. **Cards**:
   - The `Card` widget is used to create material-styled cards with elevation and rounded corners.

   Example:

```
dart

Card(
  elevation: 4,
  shape:
RoundedRectangleBorder(borderRadius:
BorderRadius.circular(10)),
  child: Padding(
    padding: EdgeInsets.all(16.0),
    child: Text('Material Card'),
  ),
)
```

By leveraging Material Design widgets, your app will automatically adopt a consistent, modern look and feel across different devices.

Real-World Example: Styling a Product Listing Screen

Let's create a simple product listing screen where we display a list of products, each with a title, description, and price. We will style the UI using Flutter's styling system to ensure it's clean, responsive, and visually appealing.

```
dart

import 'package:flutter/material.dart';

void main() {
  runApp(MyApp());
}

class MyApp extends StatelessWidget {
  @override
  Widget build(BuildContext context) {
    return MaterialApp(
      theme: ThemeData(
        primarySwatch: Colors.blue,
        textTheme: TextTheme(
          bodyText1: TextStyle(fontSize: 18),
          bodyText2: TextStyle(fontSize: 16),
          headline1:   TextStyle(fontSize:   24,
fontWeight: FontWeight.bold),
        ),
      ),
      home: ProductListScreen(),
    );
  }
```

```
}

class ProductListScreen extends StatelessWidget
{
  final List<Map<String, String>> products = [
    {'title':    'Product    1',    'description':
'Description 1', 'price': '\$20'},
    {'title':    'Product    2',    'description':
'Description 2', 'price': '\$30'},
    {'title':    'Product    3',    'description':
'Description 3', 'price': '\$40'},
  ];

  @override
  Widget build(BuildContext context) {
    return Scaffold(
      appBar:    AppBar(title:    Text('Product
Listing')),
      body: ListView.builder(
        itemCount: products.length,
        itemBuilder: (context, index) {
          return Card(
            elevation: 5,
            margin: EdgeInsets.all(10),
            shape: RoundedRectangleBorder(
              borderRadius:
BorderRadius.circular(10),
            ),
            child: Padding(
```

```
              padding: EdgeInsets.all(16.0),
              child: Column(
                crossAxisAlignment:
CrossAxisAlignment.start,
                children: <Widget>[
                  Text(
                    products[index]['title']!,
                    style:
Theme.of(context).textTheme.headline1,
                  ),
                  SizedBox(height: 8),
                  Text(

products[index]['description']!,
                    style:
Theme.of(context).textTheme.bodyText2,
                  ),
                  SizedBox(height: 8),
                  Text(
                    'Price:
${products[index]['price']}',
                    style:
Theme.of(context).textTheme.bodyText1,
                  ),
                ],
              ),
            ),
          );
        },
```

```
        ),
      );
  }
}
```

In this example:

- The `ProductListScreen` displays a list of products using a `ListView.builder`.
- Each product is displayed inside a `Card` widget, which has elevation, rounded corners, and padding.
- The product title is styled using the `headline1` style from the app's theme.
- The price and description are styled using `bodyText1` and `bodyText2`, respectively, to ensure consistency.

This screen uses Flutter's `Card`, `ListView`, `Text`, and theme customization to create a clean, responsive UI for displaying a list of products.

Conclusion

In this chapter, we covered how to style your Flutter app using various techniques, including defining global styles with themes, customizing widgets with colors, fonts, and borders, and creating consistent UIs using Material Design. We also walked through a real-world example of styling a product listing screen. With these styling techniques, you can create polished and professional-looking Flutter apps that provide a great user experience. In the next chapter, we'll dive into managing app state and building dynamic, interactive UIs.

CHAPTER 8

MANAGING APP STATE

Understanding State in Flutter Apps

State refers to the data or variables that determine the behavior and appearance of your app at any given point in time. In Flutter, managing state is crucial for ensuring that the user interface (UI) remains consistent and up-to-date when the underlying data changes.

For example, the state could be something simple, like the text inside a `TextField`, or something complex, like the contents of a shopping cart. In Flutter, state can be classified into two categories:

1. **Local state**: Data that is confined to a single widget and doesn't need to be shared.
2. **Global state**: Data that needs to be shared across multiple widgets and often affects multiple parts of the UI.

Flutter provides several ways to manage state, depending on the complexity and scope of your app.

Stateful vs. Stateless Widgets and State Management

Flutter has two types of widgets based on whether they hold mutable state:

1. **Stateless Widgets**:
   - A `StatelessWidget` is immutable, meaning it does not change after it's created. Once rendered, the widget stays the same. Stateless widgets are useful for static content that doesn't change over time.

   Example:

   ```
   dart

   class GreetingWidget extends
   StatelessWidget {
     @override
     Widget build(BuildContext context) {
       return Text('Hello, Flutter!');
     }
   }
   ```

   In this example, `GreetingWidget` is a stateless widget because the content does not change after the widget is rendered.

2. **Stateful Widgets**:

- A `StatefulWidget` can change over time, and when the state changes, the widget is rebuilt to reflect the new state. This is ideal for scenarios where the UI needs to respond to user interactions, like button presses, text input, or other dynamic changes.

Example:

```
dart

class CounterWidget extends StatefulWidget
{
  @override
  _CounterWidgetState    createState()    =>
_CounterWidgetState();
}

class      _CounterWidgetState      extends
State<CounterWidget> {
  int _counter = 0;

  void _incrementCounter() {
    setState(() {
      _counter++;
    });
  }

  @override
```

```
  Widget build(BuildContext context) {
    return Column(
      mainAxisAlignment:
MainAxisAlignment.center,
      children: <Widget>[
        Text('Counter: $_counter'),
        ElevatedButton(
          onPressed: _incrementCounter,
          child: Text('Increment'),
        ),
      ],
    );
  }
}
```

In this example, the `CounterWidget` is a stateful widget because it needs to update the UI when the counter value changes.

Introduction to Scoped Model and Provider

In Flutter, when the state needs to be shared across different parts of the app, or if you want to make state management more scalable, you can use state management libraries like **Scoped Model** and **Provider**. These libraries help manage global state efficiently and provide a clean, structured approach to state management.

1. **Scoped Model**:
   - **Scoped Model** is a simple and lightweight state management solution that allows you to define models that can be accessed across the widget tree. You can use `ScopedModel` to wrap your widget tree and pass data down through the widget hierarchy.

Example:

```
dart

class CounterModel extends Model {
  int _counter = 0;

  int get counter => _counter;

  void increment() {
    _counter++;
    notifyListeners();
  }
}

// Using ScopedModel in the widget tree
ScopedModel<CounterModel>(
  model: CounterModel(),
  child: MyApp(),
);
```

`notifyListeners()` is called when the model's state changes to inform the widgets that depend on it to rebuild.

2. **Provider**:
   - **Provider** is a more modern and flexible state management solution. It leverages **InheritedWidget** and makes it easier to manage state using **ChangeNotifier** to notify listeners when the state changes. Provider is more scalable and integrates well with other Flutter features like `Consumer` and `Selector`.

Example:

```
dart

class Counter with ChangeNotifier {
  int _counter = 0;

  int get counter => _counter;

  void increment() {
    _counter++;
    notifyListeners();
  }
}

// Using Provider in the widget tree
ChangeNotifierProvider(
```

```
    create: (context) => Counter(),
    child: MyApp(),
  );
```

In this example, the `Counter` class extends `ChangeNotifier`, and `notifyListeners()` is called when the counter value changes. Widgets that listen to this model will rebuild whenever the state changes.

Managing Global State with InheritedWidget

`InheritedWidget` is the core Flutter mechanism for propagating data down the widget tree. It is particularly useful for managing global state that needs to be shared across different parts of the app without explicitly passing data through the constructor of each widget.

How InheritedWidget Works:

- You create a custom `InheritedWidget` subclass to hold the state.
- The widget is provided to the widget tree using `InheritedWidget` and is accessed by other widgets using `of(context)`.

Example:

```dart
dart

class CounterData extends InheritedWidget {
  final int counter;
  final Widget child;

  CounterData({required this.counter, required
this.child});

  @override
  bool updateShouldNotify(covariant
InheritedWidget oldWidget) {
    return oldWidget is CounterData &&
oldWidget.counter != counter;
  }

  static CounterData? of(BuildContext context) {
    return
context.dependOnInheritedWidgetOfExactType<Coun
terData>();
  }
}

class MyCounterApp extends StatelessWidget {
  @override
  Widget build(BuildContext context) {
    return CounterData(
      counter: 0,
      child: MyHomePage(),
```

```
    );
  }
}
```

In this example, `CounterData` is an `InheritedWidget` that holds a counter value. Any widget below it in the widget tree can access the counter using `CounterData.of(context)`.

Real-World Example: Building a Todo App with State Management

Let's apply state management by building a simple Todo app. We'll manage the state of the tasks using `Provider`, allowing us to add and remove tasks from a list dynamically.

1. **Step 1: Define the Todo Model**: We'll create a `Todo` model that holds the title and completion status of each task.

   dart

   ```
   class Todo {
     String title;
     bool isCompleted;

     Todo({
       required this.title,
   ```

```
    this.isCompleted = false,
  });
}
```

2. **Step 2: Create a TodoNotifier**: This class extends `ChangeNotifier` to manage the list of tasks and notify listeners when the list changes.

```
dart

class TodoNotifier with ChangeNotifier {
  List<Todo> _todos = [];

  List<Todo> get todos => _todos;

  void addTask(String title) {
    _todos.add(Todo(title: title));
    notifyListeners();
  }

  void toggleCompletion(int index) {
    _todos[index].isCompleted =
!_todos[index].isCompleted;
    notifyListeners();
  }

  void removeTask(int index) {
    _todos.removeAt(index);
    notifyListeners();
```

```
  }
}
```

3. **Step 3: Setup Provider in the Widget Tree**: Use `ChangeNotifierProvider` to provide the `TodoNotifier` to the app.

```
dart

void main() {
  runApp(
    ChangeNotifierProvider(
      create: (context) => TodoNotifier(),
      child: MyApp(),
    ),
  );
}
```

4. **Step 4: Build the Todo UI**: The `MyHomePage` widget will display the list of todos, allow the user to add tasks, and toggle their completion status.

```
dart

class MyHomePage extends StatelessWidget {
  final TextEditingController _controller
= TextEditingController();

  @override
```

```
  Widget build(BuildContext context) {
    return Scaffold(
      appBar:   AppBar(title:   Text('Todo
App')),
      body: Column(
        children: <Widget>[
          Padding(
            padding: EdgeInsets.all(16.0),
            child: TextField(
              controller: _controller,
              decoration:
InputDecoration(labelText: 'Enter task'),
            ),
          ),
          ElevatedButton(
            onPressed: () {
              final         todo            =
_controller.text;
              if (todo.isNotEmpty) {

Provider.of<TodoNotifier>(context, listen:
false).addTask(todo);
                _controller.clear();
              }
            },
            child: Text('Add Task'),
          ),
          Expanded(
            child: Consumer<TodoNotifier>(
```

```
            builder:          (context,
todoNotifier, child) {
              return ListView.builder(
                itemCount:
todoNotifier.todos.length,
                itemBuilder:   (context,
index) {
                  final      todo       =
todoNotifier.todos[index];
                  return ListTile(
                    title:
Text(todo.title),
                    trailing:
IconButton(
                      icon:
Icon(todo.isCompleted ? Icons.check_box :
Icons.check_box_outline_blank),
                      onPressed: () {

todoNotifier.toggleCompletion(index);
                      },
                    ),
                    onLongPress: () {

todoNotifier.removeTask(index);
                    },
                  );
                },
              );
```

```
                    },
                  ),
                ),
              ],
            ),
          );
        }
      }
```

In this example:

- The user can enter tasks in the `TextField` and add them to the list.
- Tasks are displayed in a `ListView`, and users can toggle the completion status or delete tasks by long-pressing them.
- The `TodoNotifier` manages the state of the task list, and any changes trigger a rebuild of the UI using `Consumer`.

Conclusion

In this chapter, we explored the concept of state in Flutter apps and learned how to manage local and global state effectively. We compared `StatefulWidget` and `StatelessWidget` and introduced state management solutions like `ScopedModel`,

`Provider`, and `InheritedWidget`. Finally, we built a real-world Todo app with state management using `Provider` to handle the dynamic state of tasks. With this knowledge, you can manage the state of your Flutter apps efficiently, even as your app grows in complexity. In the next chapter, we will explore Flutter's layout system in more detail to help you create responsive and beautiful UIs.

CHAPTER 9

WORKING WITH EXTERNAL LIBRARIES

Using Packages and Plugins in Flutter

In Flutter, **packages** and **plugins** are essential tools that allow you to extend the functionality of your apps by leveraging pre-built solutions. Packages are collections of code that provide various features and functionality, while plugins enable access to platform-specific features (like camera, GPS, sensors, etc.).

Flutter's package ecosystem is vast and is managed through the **pub.dev** repository, where you can find and install packages and plugins that suit your app's needs.

- **Packages**: These are written in Dart and contain pure Dart code. They can be used across platforms (iOS, Android, web).
- **Plugins**: These provide access to platform-specific features using platform channels. They are often written in both Dart and the native language (Java, Kotlin for Android, Swift/Objective-C for iOS).

Using external libraries in Flutter simplifies the development process by giving you access to ready-made solutions for common tasks, like networking, authentication, UI components, and more.

Adding Dependencies to Your Flutter Project

Adding external libraries to your Flutter project is a straightforward process. You need to modify the `pubspec.yaml` file, which is used by Flutter to manage dependencies and configure your project.

Steps to Add Dependencies:

1. **Locate the `pubspec.yaml` file**: This file is located at the root of your Flutter project. It contains various settings, including the project's dependencies.
2. **Add the dependency**: To use an external package, add its name and version to the `dependencies` section of the `pubspec.yaml` file. You can find the required package details on **pub.dev**.

   Example:

   ```
   yaml

   dependencies:
   ```

```
flutter:
  sdk: flutter
http: ^0.13.3
provider: ^6.0.1
```

3. **Run `flutter pub get`**: After adding the dependencies, run the following command to download and install them:

   ```
   bash

   flutter pub get
   ```

   This will fetch the necessary packages and make them available in your project.

4. **Import the package**: Once the dependencies are added, you can import the package into your Dart files.

   Example:

   ```
   dart

   import 'package:http/http.dart' as http;
   ```

Exploring Popular Flutter Libraries for UI and Functionality

Flutter has a rich ecosystem of libraries that help you with both UI development and adding functionality to your apps. Some of the most popular libraries include:

1. **UI Libraries**:
   - **`flutter_bloc`**: A library for state management using the BLoC (Business Logic Component) pattern. It helps to manage complex state and business logic in a scalable and maintainable way.
   - **`flutter_staggered_grid_view`**: A flexible and powerful grid view that supports staggered layouts, often used for displaying images or cards.
   - **`cached_network_image`**: Used for caching images in a Flutter app. It helps to load images efficiently by caching them, preventing redundant network requests.

Example usage of `flutter_staggered_grid_view`:

```
dart

import
'package:flutter_staggered_grid_view/flut
ter_staggered_grid_view.dart';

StaggeredGridView.countBuilder(
  crossAxisCount: 4,
  itemCount: 10,
  itemBuilder: (BuildContext context, int
index) {
```

```
      return Container(
        color: Colors.blue,
        child:    Center(child:    Text('Item
$index')),
      );
    },
    staggeredTileBuilder: (int index) =>
        StaggeredTile.count(2,  index.isEven
? 1 : 2),
);
```

2. **Functionality Libraries**:
   - **`http`**: This library allows you to make HTTP requests in Flutter, which is essential for interacting with APIs.
   - **`firebase_auth`**: A Flutter plugin for Firebase authentication, providing methods for signing in with email/password, Google, Facebook, and other OAuth providers.
   - **`image_picker`**: A Flutter plugin that allows users to pick images from the gallery or take photos using the device's camera.

Example usage of `http` to fetch data from an API:

```
dart

import 'package:http/http.dart' as http;
```

```
Future<void> fetchData() async {
  final response = await
http.get(Uri.parse('https://jsonplacehold
er.typicode.com/posts'));

  if (response.statusCode == 200) {
    // If the server returns a 200 OK
response, parse the data
    print('Response body:
${response.body}');
  } else {
    // If the server does not return a 200
OK response, throw an exception
    throw Exception('Failed to load
data');
  }
}
```

Real-World Example: Integrating a Third-Party API with Flutter

In this example, we'll build a simple Flutter app that fetches data from a third-party API and displays it in a list. We'll use the `http` package to fetch data from an API and display the results in a `ListView`.

1. **Step 1: Add the `http` package**: Add the following dependency to your `pubspec.yaml` file:

   ```
   yaml

   dependencies:
     flutter:
       sdk: flutter
     http: ^0.13.3
   ```

2. **Step 2: Fetch Data from the API**: We'll use a sample API, such as **JSONPlaceholder** (https://jsonplaceholder.typicode.com), which provides free fake data for testing.

   ```
   dart

   import 'package:flutter/material.dart';
   import 'package:http/http.dart' as http;
   import 'dart:convert';

   void main() => runApp(MyApp());

   class MyApp extends StatelessWidget {
     @override
     Widget build(BuildContext context) {
       return MaterialApp(
         home: PostListScreen(),
       );
   ```

```
  }
}

class         PostListScreen         extends
StatefulWidget {
  @override
  _PostListScreenState   createState()   =>
_PostListScreenState();
}

class     _PostListScreenState     extends
State<PostListScreen> {
  List<dynamic> posts = [];

  // Fetch data from the API
  Future<void> fetchPosts() async {
    final      response      =      await
http.get(Uri.parse('https://jsonplacehold
er.typicode.com/posts'));

    if (response.statusCode == 200) {
      // If the server returns a 200 OK
response, parse the data
      setState(() {
        posts                           =
json.decode(response.body);
      });
    } else {
```

```
      throw   Exception('Failed   to   load
posts');
    }
  }

  @override
  void initState() {
    super.initState();
    fetchPosts();  // Call the fetch method
when the widget is created
  }

  @override
  Widget build(BuildContext context) {
    return Scaffold(
      appBar:                    AppBar(title:
Text('Posts')),
      body: ListView.builder(
        itemCount: posts.length,
        itemBuilder: (context, index) {
          return ListTile(
            title:
Text(posts[index]['title']),
            subtitle:
Text(posts[index]['body']),
          );
        },
      ),
    );
```

```
    }
}
```

3. **Step 3: Explanation of the Code**:
   - **`http.get()`**: Fetches the data from the API.
   - **`json.decode()`**: Parses the JSON data returned by the API into a list of posts.
   - **`setState()`**: Updates the state of the widget to rebuild the UI with the new data.
   - **`ListView.builder()`**: Dynamically generates a list of `ListTile` widgets to display each post's title and body.

Conclusion

In this chapter, we explored how to work with external libraries in Flutter, including adding dependencies, integrating third-party packages, and using popular libraries to enhance both the UI and functionality of your app. We learned how to fetch data from external APIs using the `http` package and display it in a list. This foundational knowledge will enable you to build more complex and interactive apps by leveraging the power of external libraries. In the next chapter, we will explore more advanced Flutter concepts, such as handling asynchronous tasks and managing app performance.

CHAPTER 10

MAKING YOUR APP INTERACTIVE

Introduction to Animations in Flutter

Animations are a powerful way to enhance user experience by providing smooth transitions and interactive effects. In Flutter, animations help create fluid, visually appealing UIs that respond to user input or state changes.

Flutter provides a rich set of tools to implement animations. Animations can be simple, like fading a widget in and out, or complex, like moving elements across the screen or scaling them. Whether you want subtle effects or more dynamic movements, Flutter's animation framework gives you the flexibility to bring your UI to life.

Key animation concepts in Flutter include:

- **Implicit Animations**: Simple animations that are automatically handled by Flutter.
- **Explicit Animations**: More complex animations where you have direct control over the animation behavior.

- **AnimationController**: A controller used for managing and controlling the animation's lifecycle.
- **AnimatedBuilder**: A widget that simplifies the process of building custom animations.

Implicit vs. Explicit Animations

1. **Implicit Animations**:
    - Implicit animations are simple animations that Flutter handles automatically. You don't need to specify the animation's value or duration manually. Instead, you specify the starting and ending values, and Flutter handles the rest.

Common implicit animation widgets include:

- `AnimatedContainer`: Used for animating changes to the properties of a container (e.g., size, color, margin).
- `AnimatedOpacity`: Used to animate changes in the opacity of a widget.
- `AnimatedAlign`: Used to animate the alignment of a widget.

Example:

dart

```
AnimatedContainer(
  duration: Duration(seconds: 1),
  color: _isBlue ? Colors.blue : Colors.red,
  width: _isWide ? 200 : 100,
  height: _isWide ? 100 : 200,
  child: Center(child: Text('Animated Container')),
)
```

In this example, the container's size and color animate based on the boolean values `_isBlue` and `_isWide`. The animation will automatically transition between the starting and ending values over the specified duration.

2. **Explicit Animations**:
   - Explicit animations provide more control over the animation process. You manually control the animation's duration, value changes, and behavior using an `AnimationController` and `Tween`.

Example:

dart

```
AnimationController        _controller        =
AnimationController(
  duration: const Duration(seconds: 2),
  vsync: this,
);

Tween<double> _tween = Tween(begin: 0.0,
end: 1.0);
Animation<double>         _animation          =
_tween.animate(_controller);

@override
void initState() {
  super.initState();
  _controller.forward();   //   Start   the
animation
}
```

In this example, we use an `AnimationController` to create a custom animation, and the animation progresses based on the defined `Tween` (from 0.0 to 1.0).

Building Custom Animations with AnimatedBuilder

The `AnimatedBuilder` widget allows you to create custom animations in Flutter by rebuilding the widget tree every time the animation value changes. It's a powerful tool when you want to create more intricate animations that involve multiple elements or complex transformations.

How it works:

1. You define an `AnimationController` and a `Tween` that defines the range of values for your animation.
2. You use `AnimatedBuilder` to rebuild the widget based on the animation value.

Example:

```
dart

class CustomAnimationWidget extends
StatefulWidget {
  @override
  _CustomAnimationWidgetState createState() =>
_CustomAnimationWidgetState();
}

class _CustomAnimationWidgetState extends
State<CustomAnimationWidget> with
SingleTickerProviderStateMixin {
  late AnimationController _controller;
  late Animation<double> _animation;

  @override
  void initState() {
```

```
    super.initState();
    _controller = AnimationController(
      duration: Duration(seconds: 2),
      vsync: this,
    );

    _animation = Tween<double>(begin: 0.0, end:
1.0).animate(_controller)
      ..addListener(() {
        setState(() {});
      });

    _controller.forward();    //    Start    the
animation
  }

  @override
  Widget build(BuildContext context) {
    return Scaffold(
      appBar:    AppBar(title:    Text('Custom
Animation')),
      body: Center(
        child: AnimatedBuilder(
          animation: _controller,
          builder: (context, child) {
            return Opacity(
              opacity: _animation.value,
              child: child, // Reusable child
widget
```

```
            );
          },
          child: Container(
            width: 200,
            height: 200,
            color: Colors.blue,
          ),
        ),
      ),
    );
  }

  @override
  void dispose() {
    _controller.dispose();
    super.dispose();
  }
}
```

In this example:

- We create an `AnimationController` and define an animation with `Tween<double>(begin: 0.0, end: 1.0)`, which animates the opacity of a `Container`.
- The `AnimatedBuilder` rebuilds the widget every time the animation value changes, making the `Container` fade in.

Using Flutter's AnimationController for Complex Animations

The `AnimationController` is the heart of most explicit animations in Flutter. It is used to control the animation's duration, timing, and value changes. With `AnimationController`, you can animate any type of value—whether it's a color, size, position, or rotation.

Using AnimationController:

1. **Creating and initializing**: The controller is initialized with a duration and a `TickerProvider` (`vsync`). You typically use `SingleTickerProviderStateMixin` to provide a ticker.
2. **Control the animation flow**: You can start, pause, reverse, or stop the animation.

Example:

```
dart

AnimationController _controller;
Animation<double> _animation;

@override
void initState() {
  super.initState();
```

```
  _controller = AnimationController(
    duration: const Duration(seconds: 2),
    vsync: this,
  );

  _animation  =  Tween<double>(begin:  0.0,  end:
1.0).animate(_controller)
    ..addListener(() {
      setState(() {});
    });

  _controller.forward(); // Start the animation
}

@override
Widget build(BuildContext context) {
  return AnimatedBuilder(
    animation: _controller,
    builder: (context, child) {
      return Transform.scale(
        scale: _animation.value,
        child: child, // Child widget
      );
    },
    child: Container(
      width: 200,
      height: 200,
      color: Colors.green,
    ),
```

```
  );
}
```

Here, we use the `Transform.scale` widget to animate the scale of a `Container` from 0 to 1 over a period of 2 seconds.

Real-World Example: Creating Interactive Buttons and Transitions

Let's create a simple interactive button that uses animations to scale up when pressed. We will animate the button using `AnimationController` to give it a nice feedback effect when the user taps it.

Step 1: Define the Animation:

```
dart

class AnimatedButton extends StatefulWidget {
  @override
  _AnimatedButtonState createState() =>
_AnimatedButtonState();
}

class _AnimatedButtonState extends
State<AnimatedButton> with
SingleTickerProviderStateMixin {
```

```
  late AnimationController _controller;
  late Animation<double> _animation;

  @override
  void initState() {
    super.initState();
    _controller = AnimationController(
      duration:   const   Duration(milliseconds:
200),
      vsync: this,
    );

    _animation = Tween<double>(begin: 1.0, end:
1.2).animate(
      CurvedAnimation(parent:       _controller,
curve: Curves.easeInOut),
    );
  }

  @override
  Widget build(BuildContext context) {
    return GestureDetector(
      onTap: () {
        _controller.forward();
        //  After  the  animation  is  complete,
reverse it to return the button to its original
size
        Future.delayed(Duration(milliseconds:
200), () {
```

```
          _controller.reverse();
        });
      },
      child: AnimatedBuilder(
        animation: _controller,
        builder: (context, child) {
          return Transform.scale(
            scale: _animation.value,
            child: ElevatedButton(
              onPressed: () {},
              child: Text('Tap Me'),
            ),
          );
        },
      ),
    );
  }

  @override
  void dispose() {
    _controller.dispose();
    super.dispose();
  }
}
```

Step 2: Explanation of the Code:

- The `AnimationController` controls the animation for the button. The button scales up when tapped, creating a visual feedback effect.
- The `GestureDetector` listens for the tap event, triggering the animation.
- The `Transform.scale` widget animates the scaling effect of the button.

Conclusion

In this chapter, we learned how to make your Flutter app interactive using animations. We covered implicit and explicit animations, including how to use `AnimationController` and `AnimatedBuilder` to create custom animations. We also demonstrated how to use Flutter's powerful animation system to create interactive buttons and transitions that provide engaging user experiences. With these techniques, you can create more dynamic and responsive UIs in your Flutter apps. In the next chapter, we will explore Flutter's layout system in more detail, allowing you to build complex and responsive layouts.

CHAPTER 11

NETWORKING IN FLUTTER

Fetching Data from the Internet

One of the most common features in mobile apps is the ability to fetch data from the internet. Flutter makes it easy to handle network requests through various libraries, but the most widely used is the `http` package. With this package, you can make HTTP requests to external APIs, retrieve data, and use it within your app.

To start using the `http` package, you need to add it as a dependency in your `pubspec.yaml` file:

```
yaml

dependencies:
  flutter:
    sdk: flutter
  http: ^0.13.3
```

After adding the dependency, run the following command to fetch the package:

```
bash
```

```
flutter pub get
```

Now, you can start using `http` to fetch data from a web service.

Working with HTTP Requests and APIs

Flutter provides the `http` package for making HTTP requests. You can use `http.get()`, `http.post()`, and other methods to interact with RESTful APIs. These requests are asynchronous, so you'll need to handle the responses asynchronously using `Future` and `async/await`.

Making a GET Request

To fetch data from a remote API, you typically send a GET request. Below is an example of how to use `http.get()` to fetch data.

Example:

```
dart

import 'package:http/http.dart' as http;
import 'dart:convert';

Future<void> fetchData() async {
```

```
  final          response          =          await
http.get(Uri.parse('https://jsonplaceholder.typ
icode.com/posts'));

  if (response.statusCode == 200) {
    // If the server returns a 200 OK response,
parse the JSON
    List data = json.decode(response.body);
    print(data);
  } else {
    // If the server does not return a 200 OK
response, throw an exception
    throw Exception('Failed to load data');
  }
}
```

In this example:

- `http.get()` makes an asynchronous GET request to the provided URL.
- `json.decode()` is used to convert the response body from a JSON string into a Dart object.

You can use this pattern to fetch data from any API.

Making a POST Request

For sending data to an API, you use `http.post()`.

Example:

```
dart

Future<void> sendData() async {
  final response = await http.post(

Uri.parse('https://jsonplaceholder.typicode.com
/posts'),
    headers:                          {"Content-Type":
"application/json"},
    body: json.encode({
      'title': 'foo',
      'body': 'bar',
      'userId': 1,
    }),
  );

  if (response.statusCode == 201) {
    // If the server returns a 201 Created
response, the data was sent successfully
    print('Data sent successfully');
  } else {
    throw Exception('Failed to send data');
  }
}
```

In this example, the `http.post()` method is used to send a JSON payload to the server. The server responds with a status code, which is checked to confirm whether the request was successful.

Parsing JSON Data in Flutter

Most APIs return data in **JSON format**, which needs to be parsed into a usable Dart data structure. Flutter provides the `dart:convert` library for encoding and decoding JSON.

To parse the data:

1. Use `json.decode()` to convert JSON into a Dart object (like a list or map).
2. You can then manipulate the data as needed.

Parsing JSON into Dart Objects

To handle complex JSON data, you often create a Dart model class that corresponds to the structure of the JSON data.

Example:

```
dart

class Post {
  final int id;
```

```
  final String title;
  final String body;

  Post({required this.id, required this.title,
required this.body});

  factory Post.fromJson(Map<String, dynamic>
json) {
    return Post(
      id: json['id'],
      title: json['title'],
      body: json['body'],
    );
  }
}

Future<List<Post>> fetchPosts() async {
  final response = await
http.get(Uri.parse('https://jsonplaceholder.typ
icode.com/posts'));

  if (response.statusCode == 200) {
    List jsonResponse =
json.decode(response.body);
    return jsonResponse.map((post) =>
Post.fromJson(post)).toList();
  } else {
    throw Exception('Failed to load posts');
  }
```

```
}
```

In this example:

- `Post.fromJson()` is a **factory constructor** that creates a `Post` object from the JSON data.
- `fetchPosts()` parses the JSON into a list of `Post` objects.

This approach makes it easier to handle structured data and work with it in a more type-safe manner.

Error Handling in Network Requests

Handling errors in network requests is essential to ensure that your app behaves gracefully, even when there are issues with the internet connection, the server, or the API response.

Handling HTTP Errors

When making network requests, you should always check for possible errors like network issues, invalid responses, or timeouts. The `http` package provides status codes that indicate whether the request was successful or if an error occurred.

1. **Check Status Codes**: The `statusCode` property of the `http.Response` object indicates the result of the request. The most common status codes are:
   - **200**: OK (Request was successful)
   - **201**: Created (Resource was successfully created)
   - **400**: Bad Request (The request was invalid)
   - **404**: Not Found (The requested resource could not be found)
   - **500**: Internal Server Error (Server-side issue)
2. **Try/Catch for Error Handling**: You can use a `try/catch` block to catch exceptions such as network timeouts, server errors, and invalid responses.

Example:

```
dart

Future<void> fetchData() async {
  try {
    final response = await
http.get(Uri.parse('https://jsonplaceholder.typ
icode.com/posts'));

    if (response.statusCode == 200) {
      List data = json.decode(response.body);
      print(data);
    } else {
      throw Exception('Failed to load data');
```

```
      }
    } catch (e) {
      print('Error occurred: $e');
    }
}
```

In this example, we catch any errors (such as network errors or invalid responses) and print the error message.

Real-World Example: Building a Weather App with API Integration

Let's create a simple weather app that fetches data from a weather API (such as OpenWeatherMap) and displays the temperature for a given city. We'll use the `http` package to fetch data, parse the JSON, and display the results in the app.

1. **Step 1: Register for an API Key**
    - Go to OpenWeatherMap and sign up for a free API key.
2. **Step 2: Add the `http` Package**
   Add the `http` package to your `pubspec.yaml` file:

   ```
   yaml

   dependencies:
     flutter:
   ```

```
    sdk: flutter
  http: ^0.13.3
```

Then run:

```
bash

flutter pub get
```

3. **Step 3: Fetch Weather Data**
   In your Flutter app, create a function to fetch weather data based on the city name.

```
dart

import 'package:flutter/material.dart';
import 'package:http/http.dart' as http;
import 'dart:convert';

void main() => runApp(MyApp());

class MyApp extends StatelessWidget {
  @override
  Widget build(BuildContext context) {
    return MaterialApp(
      home: WeatherScreen(),
    );
  }
}
```

```
class WeatherScreen extends StatefulWidget {
  @override
  _WeatherScreenState      createState()      =>
_WeatherScreenState();
}

class        _WeatherScreenState        extends
State<WeatherScreen> {
  String _city = 'London';
  String _temperature = '';
  String _error = '';

  Future<void> fetchWeather() async {
    final  apiKey  =  'YOUR_API_KEY';  //  Replace
with your API key
    final url =

'http://api.openweathermap.org/data/2.5/weather
?q=$_city&appid=$apiKey&units=metric';

    try {
      final        response        =        await
http.get(Uri.parse(url));

      if (response.statusCode == 200) {
        final data = json.decode(response.body);
        setState(() {
          _temperature                          =
'${data['main']['temp']}°C';
```

```
          _error = '';
        });
      } else {
        throw Exception('Failed to load weather
data');
      }
    } catch (e) {
      setState(() {
        _error = 'Error: $e';
        _temperature = '';
      });
    }
  }

  @override
  void initState() {
    super.initState();
    fetchWeather(); // Fetch weather data when
the widget is created
  }

  @override
  Widget build(BuildContext context) {
    return Scaffold(
      appBar:    AppBar(title:    Text('Weather
App')),
      body: Padding(
        padding: EdgeInsets.all(16.0),
        child: Column(
```

```
          children: <Widget>[
            TextField(
              onChanged: (text) {
                setState(() {
                  _city = text;
                });
              },
              decoration:
InputDecoration(labelText: 'Enter City'),
            ),
            SizedBox(height: 20),
            ElevatedButton(
              onPressed: fetchWeather,
              child: Text('Get Weather'),
            ),
            SizedBox(height: 20),
            _temperature.isNotEmpty
                ?              Text('Temperature:
$_temperature', style: TextStyle(fontSize: 24))
                :      Text(_error,        style:
TextStyle(fontSize: 24, color: Colors.red)),
          ],
        ),
      ),
    );
  }
}
```

Explanation:

- **API Key**: The app uses OpenWeatherMap's API, which requires an API key. Replace `'YOUR_API_KEY'` with the actual key you get from OpenWeatherMap.
- **Fetch Data**: The `fetchWeather()` function makes a `GET` request to the weather API, parses the JSON data, and extracts the temperature.
- **UI**: The UI consists of a `TextField` to input the city, a button to fetch weather data, and a `Text` widget to display the temperature or an error message.

Conclusion

In this chapter, we learned how to fetch data from the internet using the `http` package in Flutter. We explored how to make HTTP requests, parse JSON data, handle errors, and integrate external APIs into a Flutter app. Using the weather app example, we demonstrated how to fetch weather data from an external API and display it within the app. This knowledge allows you to interact with any external service and use its data to build dynamic, data-driven Flutter apps. In the next chapter, we'll explore Flutter's layout system and how to build responsive, adaptive UIs.

CHAPTER 12

LOCAL STORAGE IN FLUTTER

Introduction to Local Storage Options

Local storage is a way of saving data on the user's device, making it accessible even when the app is closed or the device is restarted. Flutter offers several options for storing data locally, each suitable for different use cases. Whether you need to store small amounts of data, complex data structures, or large datasets, Flutter has a solution for you.

Here are some common local storage options in Flutter:

1. **SharedPreferences**: Ideal for storing simple key-value pairs such as settings, flags, or user preferences.
2. **SQLite**: A relational database for storing structured data with tables, making it suitable for more complex data needs.
3. **Hive**: A lightweight and fast NoSQL database for Flutter, useful for offline storage in complex applications.
4. **File Storage**: For storing custom data or files in the device's file system.

In this chapter, we'll focus on two of the most commonly used local storage options in Flutter: **SharedPreferences** and **SQLite**.

Using SharedPreferences for Simple Data

`SharedPreferences` is a simple key-value storage system that allows you to store primitive data types (strings, integers, booleans, etc.). It is commonly used to save small pieces of data, such as user settings or authentication tokens.

To use `SharedPreferences`, you need to add the `shared_preferences` package to your `pubspec.yaml` file:

```
yaml

dependencies:
  flutter:
    sdk: flutter
  shared_preferences: ^2.0.8
```

Then, run:

```
bash

flutter pub get
```

Storing Data with SharedPreferences

Here's how you can store data using `SharedPreferences`:

```
dart

import
'package:shared_preferences/shared_preferences.
dart';

Future<void> storeData() async {
  final          prefs          =          await
SharedPreferences.getInstance();

  // Store a string value
  await prefs.setString('username', 'JohnDoe');

  // Store a boolean value
  await prefs.setBool('isLoggedIn', true);

  // Store an integer value
  await prefs.setInt('userAge', 30);

  print('Data stored successfully!');
}
```

Retrieving Data from SharedPreferences

Once the data is stored, you can retrieve it with the appropriate getter methods:

```dart
Future<void> retrieveData() async {
  final prefs = await SharedPreferences.getInstance();

  String? username = prefs.getString('username');
  bool? isLoggedIn = prefs.getBool('isLoggedIn');
  int? userAge = prefs.getInt('userAge');

  print('Username: $username');
  print('Is Logged In: $isLoggedIn');
  print('User Age: $userAge');
}
```

Removing Data

You can also remove specific data or clear all data from SharedPreferences:

```dart
// Remove a specific key
await prefs.remove('username');

// Clear all data
await prefs.clear();
```

Storing Data in SQLite with sqflite Package

For more complex data storage needs, SQLite is a great option. It's a relational database that allows you to store structured data with tables and queries. The `sqflite` package is used in Flutter to interact with SQLite databases.

To use SQLite, you need to add the `sqflite` and `path_provider` packages to your `pubspec.yaml` file:

```yaml
yaml

dependencies:
  flutter:
    sdk: flutter
  sqflite: ^2.0.0+3
  path_provider: ^2.0.6
```

Then, run:

```bash
bash

flutter pub get
```

Creating the SQLite Database

First, you'll need to define a method to create or open the SQLite database:

```
dart

import 'package:sqflite/sqflite.dart';
import
'package:path_provider/path_provider.dart';
import 'dart:io';
import 'package:path/path.dart';

class DatabaseHelper {
  static Database? _database;

  // Get the database
  Future<Database> get database async {
    if (_database != null) return _database!;

    // If the database is not created, create it
    _database = await _initDatabase();
    return _database!;
  }

  // Initialize the database
  _initDatabase() async {
    final        directory         =         await
getApplicationDocumentsDirectory();
    final     path     =     join(directory.path,
'app_database.db');
```

```
    return    openDatabase(path,    version:    1,
onCreate: (db, version) async {
      await db.execute('''
        CREATE TABLE users(
          id INTEGER PRIMARY KEY AUTOINCREMENT,
          username TEXT,
          age INTEGER
        )
      ''');
    });
  }
}
```

Inserting Data into SQLite

Next, let's define a method to insert data into the `users` table:

```
dart

Future<void>  insertUser(String  username,  int
age) async {
  final db = await database;

  await db.insert(
    'users',
    {'username': username, 'age': age},
    conflictAlgorithm:
ConflictAlgorithm.replace,
```

```
  );
  print('User inserted successfully!');
}
```

Querying Data from SQLite

You can query data from the SQLite database using the `query` method:

```
dart

Future<List<Map<String, dynamic>>> getUsers()
async {
  final db = await database;

  return await db.query('users');
}
```

Updating and Deleting Data

You can also update and delete data from SQLite:

```
dart

// Update a user
Future<void> updateUser(int id, String username,
int age) async {
  final db = await database;
```

```
  await db.update(
    'users',
    {'username': username, 'age': age},
    where: 'id = ?',
    whereArgs: [id],
  );
}

// Delete a user
Future<void> deleteUser(int id) async {
  final db = await database;

  await db.delete(
    'users',
    where: 'id = ?',
    whereArgs: [id],
  );
}
```

Real-World Example: Storing and Retrieving User Preferences

Let's put everything together by building a simple app that stores and retrieves user preferences (like a username and age) using both `SharedPreferences` and `SQLite`.

1. **Step 1: Define a Simple UI**

Here's a UI where the user can input their username and age, and save it to both `SharedPreferences` and `SQLite`.

```
dart


import 'package:flutter/material.dart';
import
'package:shared_preferences/shared_preferences.
dart';
import 'package:sqflite/sqflite.dart';
import 'database_helper.dart';

void main() => runApp(MyApp());

class MyApp extends StatelessWidget {
  @override
  Widget build(BuildContext context) {
    return MaterialApp(
      home: UserPreferencesScreen(),
    );
  }
}

class UserPreferencesScreen extends
StatefulWidget {
  @override
  _UserPreferencesScreenState createState() =>
_UserPreferencesScreenState();
}
```

```
class    _UserPreferencesScreenState    extends
State<UserPreferencesScreen> {
  final          _usernameController          =
TextEditingController();
  final            _ageController             =
TextEditingController();
  final _databaseHelper = DatabaseHelper();

  @override
  Widget build(BuildContext context) {
    return Scaffold(
      appBar:     AppBar(title:     Text('User
Preferences')),
      body: Padding(
        padding: EdgeInsets.all(16.0),
        child: Column(
          children: <Widget>[
            TextField(
              controller: _usernameController,
              decoration:
InputDecoration(labelText: 'Username'),
            ),
            TextField(
              controller: _ageController,
              decoration:
InputDecoration(labelText: 'Age'),
              keyboardType:
TextInputType.number,
```

```
            ),
            SizedBox(height: 20),
            ElevatedButton(
              onPressed: () async {
                String          username          =
_usernameController.text;
                int             age               =
int.parse(_ageController.text);

                //      Save      data      using
SharedPreferences
                final     prefs     =     await
SharedPreferences.getInstance();
                await
prefs.setString('username', username);
                await prefs.setInt('age', age);

                // Save data using SQLite
                await
_databaseHelper.insertUser(username, age);

                print('Data               saved
successfully!');
              },
              child: Text('Save Data'),
            ),
            SizedBox(height: 20),
            ElevatedButton(
              onPressed: () async {
```

```
                // Retrieve data from
SharedPreferences
                final prefs = await
SharedPreferences.getInstance();
                String? username =
prefs.getString('username');
                int? age = prefs.getInt('age');

                // Retrieve data from SQLite
                List<Map<String, dynamic>> users
= await _databaseHelper.getUsers();

                print('SharedPreferences Data:
$username, $age');
                print('SQLite Data:
${users[0]}');
              },
              child: Text('Retrieve Data'),
            ),
          ],
        ),
      ),
    );
  }
}
```

Explanation of the Code:

- **Text Fields**: Users input their username and age in `TextField` widgets.
- **Save Data**: When the "Save Data" button is pressed, the data is saved to both `SharedPreferences` and `SQLite`.
- **Retrieve Data**: When the "Retrieve Data" button is pressed, the data is retrieved from both `SharedPreferences` and `SQLite`.

Conclusion

In this chapter, we covered two important local storage options in Flutter: **SharedPreferences** and **SQLite**. We learned how to use `SharedPreferences` to store simple key-value pairs and how to work with SQLite to store and retrieve structured data in a relational database. We also built a real-world example where we stored and retrieved user preferences using both methods. Understanding these storage options will help you manage data in your Flutter apps, whether it's simple settings or more complex data structures. In the next chapter, we will explore Flutter's performance optimization techniques and best practices.

CHAPTER 13

USING FIREBASE WITH FLUTTER

Introduction to Firebase Services

Firebase is a suite of cloud-based services provided by Google for building and managing apps. It offers a wide range of services that simplify app development, such as authentication, real-time databases, cloud storage, and analytics.

Firebase integrates well with Flutter and provides a seamless way to build, scale, and manage mobile applications. Some of the most commonly used Firebase services with Flutter include:

- **Firebase Authentication**: Handles user sign-in and authentication with multiple providers (Email/Password, Google, Facebook, etc.).
- **Firebase Firestore**: A NoSQL cloud database for storing and syncing data in real-time.
- **Firebase Realtime Database**: A cloud-hosted database for syncing data in real-time between users.
- **Firebase Cloud Messaging (FCM)**: Used for sending push notifications to devices.

- **Firebase Cloud Storage**: Used for storing user-generated content like images, videos, and documents.
- **Firebase Analytics**: Provides insights into app usage, user engagement, and more.

In this chapter, we'll focus on integrating Firebase Authentication and Firebase Firestore with Flutter, and we'll demonstrate how to build a simple chat app using Firebase services.

Setting Up Firebase in a Flutter Project

Before using Firebase in your Flutter app, you need to set it up. Firebase provides an easy-to-follow setup process.

Steps to Set Up Firebase:

1. **Create a Firebase Project**:
    - Go to Firebase Console.
    - Click on "Add Project" and follow the instructions to create a new Firebase project.
2. **Add Firebase to Your Flutter App**:
    - For **Android**:
        - In the Firebase Console, select your project and click on the Android icon to add Firebase to your Android app.

        - Follow the steps to download the `google-services.json` file and place it in your `android/app` directory.
    - For **iOS**:
        - In the Firebase Console, select your project and click on the iOS icon to add Firebase to your iOS app.
        - Download the `GoogleService-Info.plist` file and place it in the `ios/Runner` directory.
3. **Install Firebase SDK for Flutter**:
    - In your `pubspec.yaml` file, add the necessary Firebase dependencies. Some commonly used Firebase packages include:

```yaml
yaml

dependencies:
  firebase_core: ^1.10.6
  firebase_auth: ^3.3.4
  cloud_firestore: ^3.1.5
```

Run `flutter pub get` to install these packages.

4. **Initialize Firebase in Your Flutter App**: In your main Flutter app file (`main.dart`), initialize Firebase before your app runs:

```
dart

import
'package:firebase_core/firebase_core.dart
';
import 'package:flutter/material.dart';

void main() async {

WidgetsFlutterBinding.ensureInitialized()
;
  await    Firebase.initializeApp();    //
Initialize Firebase
  runApp(MyApp());
}

class MyApp extends StatelessWidget {
  @override
  Widget build(BuildContext context) {
    return MaterialApp(
      home: HomeScreen(),
    );
  }
}
```

Authentication with Firebase (Email, Google, etc.)

Firebase Authentication provides backend services to help authenticate users, including simple pass-through authentication and third-party providers like Google, Facebook, and more.

Setting Up Firebase Authentication:

1. **Add Firebase Authentication Dependency**: Add `firebase_auth` to your `pubspec.yaml` file:

   yaml

   ```
   dependencies:
     firebase_auth: ^3.3.4
   ```

2. **Enable Authentication Providers**: In the Firebase Console, navigate to the **Authentication** section and enable the authentication providers you need (e.g., Email/Password, Google).
3. **Email/Password Authentication**:

   To authenticate users with email and password, use Firebase's `createUserWithEmailAndPassword` and `signInWithEmailAndPassword` methods.

   Example: **Register User**:

   dart

```
import
'package:firebase_auth/firebase_auth.dart
';

Future<User?>
registerWithEmailPassword(String    email,
String password) async {
  try {
    UserCredential userCredential = await
FirebaseAuth.instance.createUserWithEmail
AndPassword(
      email: email,
      password: password,
    );
    return userCredential.user;
  } on FirebaseAuthException catch (e) {
    print(e.message);
    return null;
  }
}
```

Example: **Sign In User**:

```
dart

Future<User?>
signInWithEmailPassword(String      email,
String password) async {
  try {
```

```
    UserCredential userCredential = await
FirebaseAuth.instance.signInWithEmailAndP
assword(
      email: email,
      password: password,
    );
    return userCredential.user;
  } on FirebaseAuthException catch (e) {
    print(e.message);
    return null;
  }
}
```

4. **Google Authentication**: Firebase also supports Google authentication, which allows users to log in with their Google account.

   To use Google sign-in, you need the `google_sign_in` package along with `firebase_auth`.

   Example:

```
dart

import
'package:firebase_auth/firebase_auth.dart
';
```

```
import
'package:google_sign_in/google_sign_in.da
rt';

Future<User?> signInWithGoogle() async {
  final    GoogleSignIn    googleSignIn    =
GoogleSignIn();
  final GoogleSignInAccount? googleUser =
await googleSignIn.signIn();
  final         GoogleSignInAuthentication?
googleAuth              =              await
googleUser?.authentication;

  final   OAuthCredential   credential    =
GoogleAuthProvider.credential(
    accessToken: googleAuth?.accessToken,
    idToken: googleAuth?.idToken,
  );

  UserCredential  userCredential  =  await
FirebaseAuth.instance.signInWithCredentia
l(credential);
  return userCredential.user;
}
```

Real-Time Database and Firestore in Firebase

Firebase provides two options for cloud-based databases:

1. **Firebase Realtime Database**: A NoSQL database that stores data as a large JSON tree and syncs data in real-time across all clients.
2. **Firebase Firestore**: A more flexible, scalable, and feature-rich NoSQL database that stores data in collections and documents.

In this chapter, we'll focus on **Firebase Firestore** due to its modern features and ease of use.

Setting Up Firestore:

Add `cloud_firestore` to your `pubspec.yaml` file:

```
yaml

dependencies:
  cloud_firestore: ^3.1.5
```

Run `flutter pub get` to install it.

Using Firestore:

Firestore is a NoSQL database that allows you to store data in documents, which are grouped into collections.

Example: **Adding Data to Firestore**:

```
dart
```

```
import
'package:cloud_firestore/cloud_firestore.dart';

Future<void> addUser(String name, int age) async
{

FirebaseFirestore.instance.collection('users').
add({
    'name': name,
    'age': age,
  }).then((value) {
    print("User Added");
  }).catchError((error) {
    print("Failed to add user: $error");
  });
}
```

Retrieving Data from Firestore:

You can retrieve data from Firestore in real-time or as a one-time fetch.

Example: **Fetching All Users**:

```
dart

Future<void> fetchUsers() async {
```

```
  QuerySnapshot    querySnapshot    =    await
FirebaseFirestore.instance.collection('users').
get();

  querySnapshot.docs.forEach((doc) {
    print(doc['name']);
    print(doc['age']);
  });
}
```

Listening for Real-Time Updates:

To listen for real-time updates to a collection or document, use `snapshots()`.

Example: **Listening for Real-Time Changes**:

```
dart

FirebaseFirestore.instance.collection('users').
snapshots().listen((snapshot) {
  snapshot.docs.forEach((doc) {
    print(doc['name']);
  });
});
```

Real-World Example: Building a Chat App with Firebase

Let's build a simple chat app using Firebase. This app will allow users to send and receive messages in real-time using Firestore.

1. **Step 1: Set Up Firestore**: Follow the setup steps mentioned earlier to enable Firestore and add it to your Flutter project.
2. **Step 2: Define the Message Model**: Create a model for the message:

```
dart

class Message {
  final String text;
  final String sender;
  final Timestamp timestamp;

  Message({required this.text, required
this.sender, required this.timestamp});

  factory Message.fromFirestore(DocumentSnapshot
doc) {
    Map data = doc.data() as Map;
    return Message(
      text: data['text'],
      sender: data['sender'],
      timestamp: data['timestamp'],
    );
  }
}
```

3. **Step 3: Create the Chat Screen**: Create a screen where users can send and receive messages.

```
dart

import
'package:cloud_firestore/cloud_firestore.dart';
import 'package:flutter/material.dart';

class ChatScreen extends StatefulWidget {
  @override
  _ChatScreenState        createState()        =>
_ChatScreenState();
}

class _ChatScreenState extends State<ChatScreen>
{
  final   TextEditingController   _controller   =
TextEditingController();

  void _sendMessage() {
    if (_controller.text.isNotEmpty) {

FirebaseFirestore.instance.collection('messages
').add({
        'text': _controller.text,
        'sender': 'User',   // You can replace
this with the actual user
```

```
        'timestamp':
FieldValue.serverTimestamp(),
      });
      _controller.clear();
    }
  }

  @override
  Widget build(BuildContext context) {
    return Scaffold(
      appBar: AppBar(title: Text('Chat App')),
      body: Column(
        children: [
          Expanded(
            child: StreamBuilder(
              stream: FirebaseFirestore.instance
                  .collection('messages')
                  .orderBy('timestamp')
                  .snapshots(),
              builder:                 (context,
AsyncSnapshot<QuerySnapshot> snapshot) {
                if (!snapshot.hasData) {
                  return          Center(child:
CircularProgressIndicator());
                }

                var          messages          =
snapshot.data!.docs.map((doc)             =>
Message.fromFirestore(doc)).toList();
```

```
                return ListView.builder(
                  itemCount: messages.length,
                  itemBuilder: (context, index)
{
                    return ListTile(
                      title:
Text(messages[index].sender),
                      subtitle:
Text(messages[index].text),
                    );
                  },
                );
              },
            ),
          ),
          Padding(
            padding: const EdgeInsets.all(8.0),
            child: TextField(
              controller: _controller,
              decoration: InputDecoration(
                hintText: 'Enter message',
                suffixIcon: IconButton(
                  icon: Icon(Icons.send),
                  onPressed: _sendMessage,
                ),
              ),
            ),
          ),
```

```
        ],
      ),
    );
  }
}
```

Explanation:

- The app displays messages in real-time using `StreamBuilder` and `snapshots()`.
- When a user types a message and presses the send button, it's stored in the `messages` collection in Firestore with the current timestamp.
- The messages are displayed in a `ListView` that updates automatically when new messages are added.

Conclusion

In this chapter, we covered how to integrate Firebase with your Flutter app, focusing on Firebase Authentication and Firestore. We explored how to authenticate users using email/password and Google, and how to store and retrieve data in Firestore in real-time. As a real-world example, we built a simple chat app that allows users to send and receive messages in real-time. Firebase services provide powerful tools for building scalable and dynamic apps, and with this knowledge, you can create robust Flutter applications backed by Firebase. In the next chapter, we will explore advanced Flutter topics to further enhance your development skills.

CHAPTER 14

FLUTTER AND DEVICE FEATURES

Accessing Device Camera and Media

One of the most commonly used features in mobile apps is the ability to access the device's camera and media files. Flutter makes it easy to work with device features like the camera, photos, and videos by using plugins such as `camera` and `image_picker`.

Using the Camera Plugin

The `camera` plugin provides access to the device's camera. With this plugin, you can capture photos, record videos, and display live camera previews.

1. **Install the Camera Plugin**: Add the `camera` dependency in your `pubspec.yaml` file:

   ```
   yaml

   dependencies:
     camera: ^0.9.4+6
   ```

Run the following command to install the plugin:

```bash
flutter pub get
```

2. **Setting up Camera**: First, you need to initialize the camera. Use `CameraController` to control the camera, and `FutureBuilder` to display the live camera preview.

Example:

```dart
import 'package:flutter/material.dart';
import 'package:camera/camera.dart';

late List<CameraDescription> cameras;
late CameraController controller;

void main() async {

WidgetsFlutterBinding.ensureInitialized()
;
  cameras = await availableCameras();
  runApp(MyApp());
}

class MyApp extends StatelessWidget {
  @override
```

```
  Widget build(BuildContext context) {
    return MaterialApp(
      home: CameraScreen(),
    );
  }
}

class CameraScreen extends StatefulWidget
{
  @override
  _CameraScreenState    createState()    =>
_CameraScreenState();
}

class      _CameraScreenState      extends
State<CameraScreen> {
  @override
  void initState() {
    super.initState();
    controller                             =
CameraController(cameras[0],
ResolutionPreset.high);
    controller.initialize().then((_) {
      setState(() {});
    });
  }

  @override
  void dispose() {
```

```
    controller.dispose();
    super.dispose();
  }

  @override
  Widget build(BuildContext context) {
    if (!controller.value.isInitialized) {
      return                    Center(child:
CircularProgressIndicator());
    }
    return Scaffold(
      appBar:  AppBar(title:  Text('Camera
Preview')),
      body: CameraPreview(controller),
    );
  }
}
```

In this example:

- We retrieve the available cameras using `availableCameras()`.
- The `CameraController` is initialized with the first available camera.
- The `CameraPreview` widget displays the live camera feed.

Using the Image Picker Plugin

The `image_picker` plugin allows you to select images from the gallery or capture images using the camera.

1. **Install the Image Picker Plugin**: Add the `image_picker` dependency in your `pubspec.yaml` file:

   yaml

   ```
   dependencies:
     image_picker: ^0.8.4+4
   ```

   Run:

   bash

   ```
   flutter pub get
   ```

2. **Picking an Image**: Use the `ImagePicker` to pick images from the gallery or capture them using the camera.

   Example:

   dart

   ```
   import 'package:flutter/material.dart';
   import
   'package:image_picker/image_picker.dart';
   ```

```
class       ImagePickerScreen       extends
StatefulWidget {
  @override
  _ImagePickerScreenState createState() =>
_ImagePickerScreenState();
}

class   _ImagePickerScreenState   extends
State<ImagePickerScreen> {
  late XFile? _image;

  Future<void> _pickImage() async {
    final     ImagePicker     _picker     =
ImagePicker();
    final    XFile?    image    =    await
_picker.pickImage(source:
ImageSource.gallery);
    setState(() {
      _image = image;
    });
  }

  @override
  Widget build(BuildContext context) {
    return Scaffold(
      appBar: AppBar(title: Text('Pick an
Image')),
      body: Center(
        child: Column(
```

```
          mainAxisAlignment:
MainAxisAlignment.center,
          children: <Widget>[
            _image == null
                ?       Text('No       image
selected.')
                :
Image.file(File(_image!.path)),
            ElevatedButton(
              onPressed: _pickImage,
              child: Text('Pick Image from
Gallery'),
            ),
          ],
        ),
      ),
    );
  }
}
```

In this example:

- We use `ImagePicker.pickImage()` to open the gallery and select an image.
- The selected image is displayed using the `Image.file()` widget.

Working with GPS and Location Services

In many apps, accessing the user's location is essential. Flutter provides the `geolocator` package, which gives you access to GPS and location services.

1. **Install the Geolocator Plugin**: Add the `geolocator` dependency to your `pubspec.yaml` file:

   ```
   yaml

   dependencies:
     geolocator: ^8.0.0
   ```

   Run:

   ```
   bash

   flutter pub get
   ```

2. **Getting the User's Current Location**: To get the user's current location, use `Geolocator.getCurrentPosition()`.

   Example:

   ```
   dart

   import 'package:flutter/material.dart';
   ```

```
import
'package:geolocator/geolocator.dart';

class         LocationScreen          extends
StatefulWidget {
  @override
  _LocationScreenState   createState()   =>
_LocationScreenState();
}

class     _LocationScreenState     extends
State<LocationScreen> {
  String _location = 'Unknown';

  Future<void> _getLocation() async {
    LocationPermission permission = await
Geolocator.requestPermission();
    if            (permission              ==
LocationPermission.whileInUse            ||
permission == LocationPermission.always) {
      Position    position     =     await
Geolocator.getCurrentPosition(desiredAccu
racy: LocationAccuracy.high);
      setState(() {
        _location        =       'Latitude:
${position.latitude},          Longitude:
${position.longitude}';
      });
    } else {
```

```
        setState(() {
          _location = 'Permission Denied';
        });
      }
    }

    @override
    Widget build(BuildContext context) {
      return Scaffold(
        appBar:   AppBar(title:   Text('Get
Location')),
        body: Center(
          child: Column(
            mainAxisAlignment:
MainAxisAlignment.center,
            children: <Widget>[
              Text('Location: $_location'),
              ElevatedButton(
                onPressed: _getLocation,
                child:   Text('Get   Current
Location'),
              ),
            ],
          ),
        ),
      );
    }
}
```

In this example:

- We use the `Geolocator.getCurrentPosition()` method to get the user's current latitude and longitude.
- The location is displayed on the screen, and we request location permission before accessing it.

Using Sensors and Motion Detection

Many mobile apps take advantage of sensors for detecting motion, orientation, and other physical changes. Flutter's `sensors_plus` package allows you to access accelerometer, gyroscope, and other device sensors.

1. **Install the Sensors Plugin**: Add `sensors_plus` to your `pubspec.yaml` file:

   ```
   yaml

   dependencies:
     sensors_plus: ^2.0.0
   ```

2. **Using Accelerometer and Gyroscope**: Example of reading accelerometer data:

   ```
   dart
   ```

```
import 'package:flutter/material.dart';
import
'package:sensors_plus/sensors_plus.dart';

class SensorScreen extends StatefulWidget
{
  @override
  _SensorScreenState    createState()    =>
_SensorScreenState();
}

class      _SensorScreenState      extends
State<SensorScreen> {
  String _accelerometerData = 'Waiting for
data...';

  @override
  void initState() {
    super.initState();

accelerometerEvents.listen((Accelerometer
Event event) {
      setState(() {
        _accelerometerData      =      'x:
${event.x}, y: ${event.y}, z: ${event.z}';
      });
    });
  }
```

```
  @override
  Widget build(BuildContext context) {
    return Scaffold(
      appBar:                AppBar(title:
Text('Accelerometer Data')),
      body: Center(
        child: Text(_accelerometerData),
      ),
    );
  }
}
```

In this example:

- We use the `accelerometerEvents` stream to listen for accelerometer data.
- The `AccelerometerEvent` provides the x, y, and z values that represent movement in three-dimensional space.

Real-World Example: Building an App with Location Tracking

Let's build a simple app that tracks the user's location in real-time. We'll use the `geolocator` package to get the current location and update it as the user moves.

1. **Setting Up the App**: We'll use the `geolocator` package to track the location, and update the UI every time the location changes.

```
dart

import 'package:flutter/material.dart';
import 'package:geolocator/geolocator.dart';

void main() => runApp(LocationTrackingApp());

class LocationTrackingApp extends
StatelessWidget {
  @override
  Widget build(BuildContext context) {
    return MaterialApp(
      home: LocationTrackingScreen(),
    );
  }
}

class LocationTrackingScreen extends
StatefulWidget {
  @override
  _LocationTrackingScreenState createState() =>
_LocationTrackingScreenState();
}
```

```
class    _LocationTrackingScreenState    extends
State<LocationTrackingScreen> {
  String _location = 'Unknown';

  void _getLocationUpdates() {
    Geolocator.getPositionStream(
      desiredAccuracy: LocationAccuracy.high,
      distanceFilter: 10,
    ).listen((Position position) {
      setState(() {
        _location          =          'Latitude:
${position.latitude},                 Longitude:
${position.longitude}';
      });
    });
  }

  @override
  void initState() {
    super.initState();
    _getLocationUpdates();
  }

  @override
  Widget build(BuildContext context) {
    return Scaffold(
      appBar:   AppBar(title:   Text('Real-Time
Location Tracking')),
      body: Center(
```

```
          child: Text(_location),
        ),
      );
    }
  }
```

In this example:

- We use `getPositionStream` to listen for real-time location updates.
- Every time the location changes, the UI updates with the new latitude and longitude.

Conclusion

In this chapter, we explored how to access various device features in Flutter, including the camera, media, GPS, and sensors. We learned how to integrate these features using plugins such as `camera`, `image_picker`, `geolocator`, and `sensors_plus`. We also built real-world examples, including an app that tracks location in real-time. These skills empower you to build apps that leverage the full potential of mobile devices, enhancing the user experience and making your app more interactive and dynamic. In the next chapter, we'll explore advanced topics in Flutter, including app performance optimization and best practices.

CHAPTER 15

HANDLING NOTIFICATIONS IN FLUTTER

Understanding Push Notifications

Push notifications are an essential feature in many mobile apps. They allow apps to send messages or alerts to users even when the app is not open, ensuring that users stay informed and engaged with timely updates. Push notifications can be used to alert users about new content, updates, reminders, promotions, or messages.

In Flutter, you can implement two main types of notifications:

1. **Push Notifications**: These notifications are sent from a remote server or cloud service (such as Firebase Cloud Messaging) and delivered to the user's device. They can be used for sending alerts, reminders, and updates in real-time.
2. **Local Notifications**: These notifications are scheduled and triggered by the app on the device itself. They do not require an internet connection and are useful for reminders, alarms, or other app-specific notifications.

In this chapter, we'll focus on how to handle both push notifications (using Firebase Cloud Messaging) and local notifications (using `flutter_local_notifications`).

Setting Up Firebase Cloud Messaging (FCM)

Firebase Cloud Messaging (FCM) is a powerful service provided by Firebase to send push notifications to users. FCM enables you to send notifications to specific devices, groups of devices, or topics.

Steps to Set Up FCM:

1. **Create a Firebase Project**:
   - Go to the Firebase Console, create a new project, and add your Flutter app to the project.
2. **Configure Firebase Cloud Messaging**:
   - In the Firebase Console, go to the **Cloud Messaging** tab under your project settings and enable FCM.
   - Add the `google-services.json` file for Android and `GoogleService-Info.plist` for iOS to your project.
   - Add the necessary dependencies in your `pubspec.yaml` file:

```
yaml

dependencies:
  firebase_core: ^1.10.6
  firebase_messaging: ^10.0.8
```

3. **Initialize Firebase in Your Flutter App**:
    - Initialize Firebase in your app by calling `Firebase.initializeApp()` in the `main.dart` file before running the app.

```
dart

import
'package:firebase_core/firebase_core.dart
';
import 'package:flutter/material.dart';

void main() async {

WidgetsFlutterBinding.ensureInitialized()
;
  await    Firebase.initializeApp();     //
Initialize Firebase
  runApp(MyApp());
}

class MyApp extends StatelessWidget {
  @override
```

```
  Widget build(BuildContext context) {
    return MaterialApp(
      home: HomeScreen(),
    );
  }
}
```

4. **Set Up Firebase Messaging**:
   - In your `main.dart`, initialize the `FirebaseMessaging` instance and configure it to handle background and foreground notifications.

Example:

```
dart

import
'package:firebase_messaging/firebase_mess
aging.dart';

class MyApp extends StatefulWidget {
  @override
  _MyAppState         createState()         =>
_MyAppState();
}

class _MyAppState extends State<MyApp> {
```

```
  FirebaseMessaging _firebaseMessaging =
FirebaseMessaging.instance;

  @override
  void initState() {
    super.initState();

_firebaseMessaging.subscribeToTopic('news
');

_firebaseMessaging.getInitialMessage().th
en((message) {
      if (message != null) {
        print('Notification clicked:
$message');
      }
    });


FirebaseMessaging.onMessage.listen((Remot
eMessage message) {
      if (message.notification != null) {
        print('Foreground notification:
${message.notification!.title}');
      }
    });
```

```
FirebaseMessaging.onMessageOpenedApp.list
en((RemoteMessage message) {
      print('Notification         clicked:
${message.data}');
    });
  }

  @override
  Widget build(BuildContext context) {
    return MaterialApp(
      home: Scaffold(
        appBar: AppBar(
          title:       Text('FCM       Push
Notifications'),
        ),
        body:   Center(child:   Text('Push
Notification Example')),
      ),
    );
  }
}
```

5. **Sending a Push Notification**:
   - You can send push notifications from Firebase Console by navigating to the **Cloud Messaging** tab and sending a test message to a specific device or topic.

- o Alternatively, you can send notifications programmatically using Firebase Admin SDK or any backend service.

Managing Local Notifications with flutter_local_notifications

In addition to push notifications, local notifications are useful when you want to show notifications to users based on app data or user actions (such as reminders or alerts).

The `flutter_local_notifications` package is a versatile Flutter package for displaying local notifications.

Steps to Set Up Local Notifications:

1. **Install the flutter_local_notifications Package**: Add the `flutter_local_notifications` package to your `pubspec.yaml` file:

   ```
   yaml

   dependencies:
     flutter:
       sdk: flutter
     flutter_local_notifications: ^9.1.4
   ```

2. **Configure Local Notifications**: Set up local notifications by initializing the notification plugin and configuring the settings for Android and iOS.

   Example:

```
dart

import 'package:flutter/material.dart';
import
'package:flutter_local_notifications/flut
ter_local_notifications.dart';

void main() => runApp(MyApp());

class MyApp extends StatelessWidget {
  @override
  Widget build(BuildContext context) {
    return MaterialApp(
      home: NotificationScreen(),
    );
  }
}

class      NotificationScreen      extends
StatefulWidget {
  @override
  _NotificationScreenState   createState()
=> _NotificationScreenState();
```

```
}

class _NotificationScreenState extends
State<NotificationScreen> {
  FlutterLocalNotificationsPlugin
flutterLocalNotificationsPlugin =
FlutterLocalNotificationsPlugin();

  @override
  void initState() {
    super.initState();
    initializeNotifications();
  }

  // Initialize the notifications
  void initializeNotifications() async {
    var initializationSettingsAndroid =

AndroidInitializationSettings('app_icon')
;
    var initializationSettings =
        InitializationSettings(android:
initializationSettingsAndroid);

    await
flutterLocalNotificationsPlugin.initializ
e(initializationSettings);
  }
```

```
  // Show a simple notification
  Future<void> showNotification() async {
    var         androidDetails          =
AndroidNotificationDetails(
      'channel_id',
      'channel_name',
      importance: Importance.max,
      priority: Priority.high,
    );
    var         platformDetails          =
NotificationDetails(android:
androidDetails);

    await
flutterLocalNotificationsPlugin.show(
      0,
      'Test Notification',
      'This is a test notification',
      platformDetails
    );
  }

  @override
  Widget build(BuildContext context) {
    return Scaffold(
      appBar:  AppBar(title:  Text('Local
Notifications')),
      body: Center(
        child: ElevatedButton(
```

```
              onPressed: showNotification,
              child:                    Text('Show
Notification'),
            ),
          ),
        );
      }
    }
```

In this example:

- We initialize the `flutter_local_notifications` plugin with basic settings.
- The `showNotification` method is used to display a local notification with custom Android settings (e.g., importance and priority).

Real-World Example: Building an App with Push Notifications

Let's build an app that demonstrates how to use both push notifications (via Firebase) and local notifications. We will create a simple to-do list app that:

- Sends push notifications when a task is added.
- Uses local notifications for reminders when a task is due.

1. **Set Up Firebase for Push Notifications**: Follow the steps outlined earlier to integrate Firebase and set up Firebase Cloud Messaging (FCM).
2. **Add Local Notifications**: Use `flutter_local_notifications` to display a reminder when a task is due.
3. **UI for the App**: Create a basic UI where users can add tasks and set reminders.

Example of the full app logic:

```
dart


import 'package:flutter/material.dart';
import
'package:firebase_messaging/firebase_messaging.
dart';
import
'package:flutter_local_notifications/flutter_lo
cal_notifications.dart';

void main() => runApp(MyApp());

class MyApp extends StatelessWidget {
  @override
  Widget build(BuildContext context) {
    return MaterialApp(
      home: TodoScreen(),
    );
```

```
  }
}

class TodoScreen extends StatefulWidget {
  @override
  _TodoScreenState        createState()        =>
_TodoScreenState();
}

class _TodoScreenState extends State<TodoScreen>
{
  FlutterLocalNotificationsPlugin
flutterLocalNotificationsPlugin                =
FlutterLocalNotificationsPlugin();
  FirebaseMessaging     _firebaseMessaging     =
FirebaseMessaging.instance;

  @override
  void initState() {
    super.initState();
    initializeNotifications();

_firebaseMessaging.getInitialMessage().then((me
ssage) {
      if (message != null) {
        showLocalNotification('New  Task',  'You
have a new task');
      }
    });
```

```
FirebaseMessaging.onMessage.listen((message) {

showLocalNotification(message.notification!.tit
le!, message.notification!.body!);
    });
  }

  // Initialize notifications
  void initializeNotifications() async {
    var              androidDetails              =
AndroidInitializationSettings('app_icon');
    var         initializationSettings          =
InitializationSettings(android: androidDetails);
    await
flutterLocalNotificationsPlugin.initialize(init
ializationSettings);
  }

  // Show local notification
  Future<void>      showLocalNotification(String
title, String body) async {
    var              androidDetails              =
AndroidNotificationDetails(
      'channel_id',
      'channel_name',
      importance: Importance.max,
      priority: Priority.high,
    );
```

```
    var              platformDetails              =
NotificationDetails(android: androidDetails);
    await
flutterLocalNotificationsPlugin.show(0,   title,
body, platformDetails);
  }

  // Handle adding a new task
  void addTask(String task) {
    // Show push notification to all users

FirebaseMessaging.instance.subscribeToTopic('to
dos');
    FirebaseMessaging.instance.send(
      Message(
        notification:  Notification(title:  'New
Task', body: task),
        topic: 'todos',
      ),
    );

    // Show local notification for the user
    showLocalNotification('New    Task',    'You
added: $task');
  }

  @override
  Widget build(BuildContext context) {
    return Scaffold(
```

```
      appBar:      AppBar(title:      Text('Task
Notifications')),
      body: Center(
        child: ElevatedButton(
          onPressed: () {
            addTask('Finish homework');
          },
          child: Text('Add Task'),
        ),
      ),
    );
  }
}
```

In this example:

- The app listens for new push notifications and displays local notifications for all events.
- When a new task is added, both a push notification and a local notification are triggered.

Conclusion

In this chapter, we explored how to handle notifications in Flutter. We learned how to set up **Firebase Cloud Messaging (FCM)** for push notifications, and how to use the **flutter_local_notifications** package to manage local notifications. By combining these two types of notifications, you can keep users engaged with your app through real-time updates and reminders. We also created a real-world example by building a simple to-do list app with both push and local notifications. In the next chapter, we will delve into further Flutter capabilities, such as app performance optimization.

CHAPTER 16

TESTING YOUR FLUTTER APP

Introduction to Flutter Testing Framework

Testing is an essential part of the software development process that helps ensure the reliability, performance, and correctness of your app. Flutter provides a rich testing framework that supports multiple types of testing, including **unit tests**, **widget tests**, and **integration tests**.

Flutter's testing framework is built on top of the `test` package and includes specific tools and libraries for widget testing, which is essential for building user interfaces.

Key Types of Tests in Flutter:

1. **Unit Tests**: These tests check individual pieces of logic (functions, methods, or classes) to ensure they work correctly in isolation.
2. **Widget Tests**: These tests verify the UI components and interactions within a specific widget, ensuring that your widgets render as expected and respond correctly to user input.

3. **Integration Tests**: These tests simulate user interactions across multiple widgets and check how different parts of the app interact together, ensuring that the entire app works as intended.

In this chapter, we will focus on writing **unit tests** and **widget tests**, as well as debugging with **Flutter DevTools**.

Writing Unit Tests and Widget Tests

Unit Tests

Unit tests are used to test the smallest units of code—usually individual functions or methods. They are useful for testing business logic, data manipulation, and other non-UI components of the app.

1. **Setting Up Unit Tests**: To write unit tests, you need to add the `test` package to your `pubspec.yaml` file:

   ```
   yaml

   dependencies:
     flutter:
       sdk: flutter

   dev_dependencies:
   ```

```
  test: ^1.16.0
```

Run the following command to install the test package:

```bash
flutter pub get
```

2. **Writing a Simple Unit Test**: Suppose you have a function that adds two numbers. You can write a unit test to check if the function returns the correct result.

   Example:

```dart
int add(int a, int b) {
  return a + b;
}

void main() {
  test('Test add function', () {
    // Arrange
    int a = 2;
    int b = 3;

    // Act
    int result = add(a, b);

    // Assert
```

```
        expect(result, 5);
    });
}
```

In this example:

- The `test()` function defines a test case.
- `expect()` is used to check that the result of the `add()` function equals the expected value (5).

3. **Running Unit Tests**: To run the tests, use the following command in the terminal:

```
bash

flutter test
```

Widget Tests

Widget tests focus on testing the UI components and interactions. These tests are particularly useful for verifying that your widgets are rendered correctly and behave as expected when interacted with by the user.

1. **Setting Up Widget Tests**: Widget tests require a test environment where widgets can be rendered and interacted with. You need to import `flutter_test` and define a testable widget in your app.

Example of testing a widget:

```
dart

import 'package:flutter/material.dart';
import
'package:flutter_test/flutter_test.dart';

void main() {
  testWidgets('Test Widget', (WidgetTester
tester) async {
    // Build the widget
    await tester.pumpWidget(MaterialApp(
      home: Scaffold(
        body: ElevatedButton(
          onPressed: () {},
          child: Text('Click Me'),
        ),
      ),
    ));

    // Verify that the button exists
    expect(find.text('Click          Me'),
findsOneWidget);

    // Simulate a tap on the button
    await      tester.tap(find.text('Click
Me'));

    // Verify the result after tapping
```

```
    // Add further checks to verify the button behavior
  });
}
```

In this example:

- `testWidgets()` is used to define a widget test.
- `tester.pumpWidget()` builds the widget tree and renders it in the test environment.
- `find.text()` is used to find widgets by their text.
- `tester.tap()` simulates a user tap on the widget.

2. **Running Widget Tests**: Widget tests can be run using the same `flutter test` command that you use for unit tests:

```
bash

flutter test
```

Debugging with Flutter DevTools

Flutter DevTools is a suite of performance and debugging tools that help you understand and debug your Flutter applications.

DevTools provides tools for inspecting widget trees, viewing performance data, monitoring network requests, and more.

Using Flutter DevTools for Debugging:

1. **Install DevTools**: To use DevTools, ensure that you have it installed:

   ```
   bash

   flutter pub global activate devtools
   ```

2. **Launch DevTools**: You can launch DevTools from the command line by running:

   ```
   bash

   flutter pub global run devtools
   ```

   This will open the DevTools interface in your browser. You can also access DevTools directly from within Visual Studio Code or Android Studio if you're using those IDEs.

3. **Using DevTools Features**: DevTools provides a variety of features:
   - **Widget Inspector**: Inspect the widget tree to check if your widgets are laid out and rendered correctly.

- **Performance View**: Monitor the app's performance, including frame rendering times and CPU usage.
- **Memory View**: Track memory usage to identify potential memory leaks or excessive memory consumption.
- **Network Tab**: View network requests made by the app to analyze API calls or other network activity.

Real-World Example: Writing Tests for a Flutter App

Let's build a simple counter app and write tests for it. This app will have a button that increments a counter and displays the count.

Step 1: Build the Counter App

```
dart

import 'package:flutter/material.dart';

void main() {
  runApp(MyApp());
}

class MyApp extends StatelessWidget {
```

```
  @override
  Widget build(BuildContext context) {
    return MaterialApp(
      home: CounterScreen(),
    );
  }
}

class CounterScreen extends StatefulWidget {
  @override
  _CounterScreenState      createState()       =>
_CounterScreenState();
}

class          _CounterScreenState          extends
State<CounterScreen> {
  int _counter = 0;

  void _incrementCounter() {
    setState(() {
      _counter++;
    });
  }

  @override
  Widget build(BuildContext context) {
    return Scaffold(
      appBar:    AppBar(title:    Text('Counter
App')),
```

```
      body: Center(
        child: Column(
          mainAxisAlignment:
MainAxisAlignment.center,
          children: <Widget>[
            Text('Counter: $_counter'),
            ElevatedButton(
              onPressed: _incrementCounter,
              child: Text('Increment'),
            ),
          ],
        ),
      ),
    );
  }
}
```

Step 2: Write Unit Tests for the Counter App

Now, let's write a simple unit test for the `_incrementCounter` method to ensure it works correctly.

```
dart

import 'package:flutter_test/flutter_test.dart';
import 'package:counter_app/main.dart';

void main() {
  test('Counter increments by 1', () {
```

```
    final app = MyApp();
    final counterScreen = app.createState();

    // Verify initial counter value
    expect(counterScreen._counter, 0);

    // Call _incrementCounter and verify the new
value
    counterScreen._incrementCounter();
    expect(counterScreen._counter, 1);
  });
}
```

In this test:

- We check that the initial counter value is `0`.
- We simulate a click on the increment button by calling `_incrementCounter` directly and verify that the counter increments to `1`.

Step 3: Write Widget Tests for the Counter App

Next, let's write a widget test to check if the counter is incrementing properly when the button is pressed.

```
dart

import 'package:flutter/material.dart';
import 'package:flutter_test/flutter_test.dart';
```

```
import 'package:counter_app/main.dart';

void main() {
  testWidgets('Counter increments when the button is pressed', (WidgetTester tester) async {
    // Build the widget
    await tester.pumpWidget(MyApp());

    // Verify initial counter value
    expect(find.text('Counter: 0'), findsOneWidget);

    // Tap the increment button
    await tester.tap(find.text('Increment'));
    await tester.pump();

    // Verify the counter value has incremented
    expect(find.text('Counter: 1'), findsOneWidget);
  });
}
```

In this test:

- We use `tester.pumpWidget()` to render the app.
- We use `find.text()` to locate the initial and updated counter text.

- We simulate a tap on the "Increment" button and then check that the counter updates correctly.

Conclusion

In this chapter, we explored Flutter's testing framework and learned how to write unit tests and widget tests. We also introduced **Flutter DevTools** for debugging and performance monitoring. By writing tests for our simple counter app, we demonstrated how to ensure the correctness of individual logic (unit tests) and UI interactions (widget tests). Testing is a crucial part of software development, and Flutter's testing tools allow you to build reliable and maintainable apps. In the next chapter, we will explore performance optimization techniques and best practices to make your Flutter apps run smoothly.

CHAPTER 17

DEBUGGING AND PERFORMANCE OPTIMIZATION

Using Flutter DevTools for Debugging

Flutter DevTools is a powerful suite of performance and debugging tools designed to help developers analyze and optimize their Flutter applications. It provides a set of tools for inspecting the app's widget tree, tracking performance, checking network activity, and debugging UI issues.

Key Features of Flutter DevTools:

1. **Widget Inspector**: The widget inspector allows you to inspect the widget tree and view detailed information about each widget, such as its properties, state, and layout.
2. **Performance View**: This tool helps track the performance of the app, including frame rendering times and CPU usage.
3. **Memory View**: The memory view allows you to track memory usage and helps identify potential memory leaks or areas where memory usage can be optimized.

4. **Network View**: The network view displays network activity and API calls made by your app.
5. **Logging and Debugging**: DevTools enables the debugging of network requests, exceptions, and logs generated by the app.

Setting Up DevTools:

1. **Install DevTools**: First, ensure that DevTools is installed by running the following command:

   ```
   bash

   flutter pub global activate devtools
   ```

2. **Launch DevTools**: After the installation, launch DevTools with the command:

   ```
   bash

   flutter pub global run devtools
   ```

   DevTools will open in your browser and can be accessed from within Visual Studio Code, Android Studio, or directly from the command line.

3. **Inspect the Widget Tree**: The widget inspector in DevTools provides a real-time view of the widget tree. It

can help you visualize the structure of your app and ensure that widgets are laid out as expected.

Identifying and Resolving Performance Bottlenecks

Performance is a critical aspect of mobile app development. Flutter provides several tools to identify and resolve performance bottlenecks, helping you keep your app fast and responsive.

Common Performance Bottlenecks:

1. **Jank (Frame Drops)**: Jank occurs when the app's frame rate drops below the optimal target (usually 60 frames per second), causing visible stuttering or lag.
2. **Excessive CPU or Memory Usage**: High CPU usage can make your app feel sluggish, while excessive memory usage can lead to crashes or slowdowns due to out-of-memory errors.

Using the Performance View in DevTools:

The Performance view in Flutter DevTools provides a detailed timeline of your app's frame rendering. You can track the amount of time it takes to render each frame, and identify any spikes or delays in the rendering process.

1. **Open the Performance Tab**: Launch DevTools, and open the "Performance" tab to monitor your app's performance.
2. **Track Jank**: The timeline will show you when the app misses a frame (jank), and you can drill down to see which operations caused the delay.
3. **Analyze Frame Rendering**: Use the timeline to analyze the time it takes to render a frame and check for any operations that might be taking too long.

Optimizing Frame Rendering:

To reduce jank and optimize frame rendering:

1. **Minimize Heavy Computation on the Main Thread**: Heavy computations or complex UI rendering can block the main thread and cause jank. Offload heavy tasks to background threads or isolate workers.
2. **Use `RepaintBoundary`**: The `RepaintBoundary` widget can be used to isolate parts of the widget tree that need to be redrawn. This can help optimize rendering performance by minimizing the area that needs to be repainted.

Example of using `RepaintBoundary`:

dart

```
RepaintBoundary(
  child: YourWidget(),
)
```

3. **Use `ListView.builder` for Large Lists**: If you have a large list of items to display, use `ListView.builder` instead of `ListView` to render only the visible items. This reduces memory consumption and rendering time.

Optimizing App Startup Time and Memory Usage

Optimizing your app's startup time and memory usage is key to providing a smooth user experience. Slow app startup times and high memory usage can frustrate users and lead to higher app uninstallation rates.

Optimizing Startup Time:

1. **Lazy Loading**: Load only the essential components during the initial startup, and defer loading other components until necessary.
2. **Reduce Dependencies**: Avoid loading unnecessary packages or dependencies at startup. Only load what is required for the first screen or operation.

3. **Use `async` and `await` Efficiently**: Use asynchronous programming techniques to load resources in the background and prevent blocking the UI thread.

Example:

```
dart

Future<void> initializeApp() async {
  await   Future.delayed(Duration(seconds:   1));
// Simulate network request
  runApp(MyApp());     //  Start  the  app  after
initialization
}
```

Optimizing Memory Usage:

1. **Release Unused Resources**: Ensure that resources like images, network connections, or large data objects are properly disposed of when not in use.
2. **Avoid Memory Leaks**: Monitor for memory leaks by using DevTools' memory view to identify uncollected resources.
3. **Limit Image and Asset Sizes**: Use appropriately sized images and assets to reduce memory usage.

Real-World Example: Debugging and Optimizing a Flutter App

Let's look at a simple example where we optimize a Flutter app's performance and debug it using DevTools.

Step 1: Build a Simple App

Let's say we have an app with a long list of items and some heavy computation on the main thread.

```
dart

import 'package:flutter/material.dart';

void main() {
  runApp(MyApp());
}

class MyApp extends StatelessWidget {
  @override
  Widget build(BuildContext context) {
    return MaterialApp(
      home: LongListScreen(),
    );
  }
}

class LongListScreen extends StatelessWidget {
```

```
  final         List<String>        items        =
List.generate(10000, (index) => 'Item $index');

  @override
  Widget build(BuildContext context) {
    return Scaffold(
      appBar: AppBar(title: Text('Long List')),
      body: ListView.builder(
        itemCount: items.length,
        itemBuilder: (context, index) {
          // Simulate heavy computation
          for (int i = 0; i < 1000000; i++) {
            // Dummy computation to simulate lag
          }
          return ListTile(
            title: Text(items[index]),
          );
        },
      ),
    );
  }
}
```

In this example, we generate a list of 10,000 items and perform heavy computation (a loop) inside the `itemBuilder`, which will cause jank and poor performance.

Step 2: Debugging Performance with DevTools

1. **Run the App with DevTools**: Launch your app and start DevTools using the command:

   bash

   ```
   flutter pub global run devtools
   ```

2. **Inspect the Widget Tree**: Use the Widget Inspector to ensure that the widget tree is being rendered as expected. Check for unnecessary widgets or components that can be optimized.
3. **Analyze the Performance Timeline**: Open the **Performance** tab in DevTools and look at the rendering timeline to see where the app is spending time. You will notice that the frame rate drops due to the heavy computation inside the `itemBuilder`.

Step 3: Optimize the Code

To improve the performance, we can move the heavy computation outside the `itemBuilder` and use `ListView.builder` to render the list efficiently.

1. **Optimize Computation**: Instead of running the computation inside the `itemBuilder`, we can use a background isolate or simply avoid unnecessary loops.

dart

```
class OptimizedLongListScreen extends StatelessWidget {
  final List<String> items = List.generate(10000, (index) => 'Item $index');

  @override
  Widget build(BuildContext context) {
    return Scaffold(
      appBar: AppBar(title: Text('Optimized Long List')),
      body: ListView.builder(
        itemCount: items.length,
        itemBuilder: (context, index) {
          return ListTile(
            title: Text(items[index]),
          );
        },
      ),
    );
  }
}
```

2. **Use `ListView.builder` Efficiently**: The `ListView.builder` only builds the visible items, which improves memory usage and performance. By avoiding heavy computations inside the `itemBuilder`, we ensure smooth scrolling and rendering.

3. **Test the Optimized App**: After making these changes, rerun the app and check the performance again using DevTools. You should notice improved frame rates and reduced jank.

Conclusion

In this chapter, we learned how to use **Flutter DevTools** for debugging and optimizing Flutter apps. We explored common performance bottlenecks like jank and excessive CPU usage and demonstrated how to optimize app startup time and memory usage. We also wrote a real-world example where we debugged and optimized a Flutter app with a long list of items, showing how to use DevTools to track performance issues and make improvements. By following these techniques, you can ensure that your Flutter apps run smoothly and provide the best user experience. In the next chapter, we will explore advanced Flutter topics like building custom plugins and handling background tasks.

CHAPTER 18

DEPLOYING YOUR APP TO THE APP STORES

Preparing for iOS and Android Deployment

Once you've built and tested your Flutter app, the next step is to prepare it for deployment to the **Google Play Store** and the **Apple App Store**. Before deploying, you need to ensure that your app meets the requirements for both platforms, is optimized, and follows best practices.

1. Setting Up for iOS Deployment

For iOS deployment, you need to have a **Mac** with Xcode installed. You will also need to have an **Apple Developer Account** to publish your app on the App Store.

Steps to prepare your app for iOS deployment:

1. **Create an App ID and Provisioning Profile**:
    - Go to the **Apple Developer Console** and create a new App ID for your app.

   - Set up a **Provisioning Profile** in Xcode to sign your app.
2. **Ensure the iOS App Configuration**:
   - In the `ios/Runner/Info.plist` file, you should specify key information about your app, such as permissions, app settings, and supported devices.
3. **Set the Deployment Target**:
   - Set the deployment target to ensure your app works on the supported iOS versions.
4. **Test on Real Devices**:
   - Before submission, test your app on actual iOS devices to ensure that everything functions properly, including performance and UI.

2. Setting Up for Android Deployment

For Android, you need an **Android Developer Account** to publish your app on the Google Play Store. Additionally, you must create a **release key** to sign your app.

Steps to prepare your app for Android deployment:

1. **Generate a Signed APK or AAB**:
   - Use the `flutter build` command to generate a release APK or AAB (Android App Bundle),

which is required for uploading to the Google Play Store.

```
bash

flutter build apk --release
```

or

```
bash

flutter build appbundle --release
```

2. **Configure the Android App Settings**:
   - In `android/app/src/main/AndroidManifest.xml`, ensure your app's settings (permissions, version codes, etc.) are set up correctly.
3. **Test on Real Devices**:
   - Always test your app on various Android devices to ensure compatibility across different screen sizes, Android versions, and device types.

Configuring App Icons, Splash Screens, and Branding

Before submitting your app to the stores, you should make sure that your app has the correct icons, splash screens, and branding to make it look professional and match your app's design guidelines.

1. App Icons:

App icons are essential for branding and user recognition. You need to add a high-quality app icon in various sizes to support both iOS and Android.

For Android:

- The icon should be added to `android/app/src/main/res/` in various drawable folders (e.g., `drawable-mdpi`, `drawable-hdpi`, etc.).

For iOS:

- The icon should be added to the `ios/Runner/Assets.xcassets/AppIcon.appiconset/` folder.

You can use the `flutter_launcher_icons` package to automate the process of generating and setting icons for both platforms.

Add the dependency:

```
yaml
```

```
dev_dependencies:
  flutter_launcher_icons: ^0.9.2

flutter_icons:
  android: true
  ios: true
  image_path: "assets/icons/app_icon.png"
```

Then run the following command to generate the icons:

```
bash

flutter pub get
flutter pub run flutter_launcher_icons:main
```

2. Splash Screens:

Splash screens are displayed when the app is launched, giving users a smooth transition into the app. Flutter supports customizing splash screens for both platforms.

For Android:

- Customize the splash screen by modifying the `android/app/src/main/res/drawable/launch_background.xml` file.

For iOS:

- The splash screen is configured in `ios/Runner/LaunchScreen.storyboard`.

You can use packages like `flutter_native_splash` to easily configure and generate splash screens for both Android and iOS.

Add the dependency to `pubspec.yaml`:

```
yaml

dev_dependencies:
  flutter_native_splash: ^2.0.3

flutter_native_splash:
  color: "#ffffff"
  image: "assets/images/splash.png"
```

Then run:

```
bash

flutter pub get
flutter pub run flutter_native_splash:create
```

Publishing to Google Play Store and Apple App Store

After preparing your app, it's time to publish it. Both the **Google Play Store** and **Apple App Store** have specific guidelines and processes for submitting apps.

1. Publishing to the Google Play Store:

1. **Create a Developer Account**:
   - Go to the Google Play Console and create a developer account. There is a one-time registration fee.
2. **Prepare the App for Release**:
   - Ensure that the version code and version name are updated in the `android/app/build.gradle` file:

     ```
     gradle

     versionCode: 1
     versionName: "1.0.0"
     ```
3. **Upload the APK or AAB**:
   - In the Google Play Console, create a new app and upload the release APK or AAB generated from the `flutter build` command.
4. **Fill in the App Details**:
   - Add necessary details such as app description, screenshots, category, and pricing.
5. **Submit for Review**:

- After filling out all the required information, submit the app for review. Google typically takes a few days to review and approve the app.

2. Publishing to the Apple App Store:

1. **Create a Developer Account**:
    - Go to the Apple Developer Program and sign up for a developer account. There is an annual fee for enrollment.
2. **Prepare the App for Release**:
    - In Xcode, set the app's build version and ensure that it matches the version in the `ios/Runner/Info.plist` file.
3. **Upload the IPA**:
    - Use Xcode's `Archive` feature to build and upload your app to the App Store. You can do this by selecting your app's target and clicking on `Product > Archive`.
4. **Fill in the App Details**:
    - In the App Store Connect, create a new app listing and add the necessary metadata, such as screenshots, app description, and pricing.
5. **Submit for Review**:
    - After filling out the app details, submit your app for review. The review process can take a few days, and Apple may require additional

information if the app doesn't meet their guidelines.

Handling Versioning and App Updates

Managing app versions and updates is crucial to ensure smooth user experiences when releasing new features or bug fixes.

1. Versioning:

- **Android**: The version code (an integer) and version name (a string) should be updated in the `android/app/build.gradle` file:

  ```
  gradle

  versionCode 2
  versionName "1.1.0"
  ```

  - The `versionCode` is incremented with every new release, while `versionName` represents the version that users will see.
- **iOS**: The version number and build number are set in the `ios/Runner/Info.plist` file:

  ```
  xml
  ```

```
<key>CFBundleShortVersionString</key>
<string>1.1.0</string>
<key>CFBundleVersion</key>
<string>2</string>
```

2. Handling App Updates:

- **Android**: When updating your app, ensure that the version code is incremented. After submitting the update, users will be prompted to update the app via the Play Store.
- **iOS**: Similar to Android, increment the version number and build number. After submitting the update, users will be notified to update the app via the App Store.

Real-World Example: Publishing Your First Flutter App

Let's walk through the steps of publishing a simple Flutter app to both the **Google Play Store** and the **Apple App Store**.

1. **Prepare the App**:
   - Complete the app's UI and functionality.
   - Test the app thoroughly on both Android and iOS devices.
2. **Set App Version and Build**:

   - For Android, update the version code and version name in `android/app/build.gradle`.
   - For iOS, update the version number and build number in `ios/Runner/Info.plist`.
3. **Generate the Release Build**:
   - For Android, run the following command to build the APK or AAB:

     ```
     bash

     flutter build appbundle --release
     ```

   - For iOS, archive the app using Xcode and create an IPA file.
4. **Upload to App Stores**:
   - For the Google Play Store, upload the AAB file through the Play Console.
   - For the Apple App Store, upload the IPA file using Xcode and fill out the necessary details in App Store Connect.
5. **Submit for Review**:
   - Submit the app for review and wait for approval. Once approved, the app will be live on the respective app stores.

Conclusion

In this chapter, we discussed the steps required to prepare, configure, and deploy your Flutter app to both the **Google Play Store** and **Apple App Store**. We covered how to configure app icons, splash screens, and branding, and how to manage versioning and app updates. By following these steps, you can successfully publish your first Flutter app and share it with users around the world. In the next chapter, we will delve into advanced topics, such as building custom plugins and handling background tasks in Flutter.

CHAPTER 19

FLUTTER FOR WEB AND DESKTOP APPS

Introduction to Flutter for Web

Flutter started as a mobile-first framework, but with the introduction of Flutter for Web, it has evolved into a cross-platform development solution that supports not only iOS and Android but also web and desktop platforms. Flutter for Web allows developers to use the same codebase to create applications that run in a browser, making it easier to maintain and deliver cross-platform experiences.

Advantages of Flutter for Web:

- **Single Codebase**: You can share the same code for your mobile, web, and desktop apps, making the development process more efficient.
- **Rich UI Components**: Flutter provides a comprehensive set of widgets and tools for building highly interactive and responsive user interfaces on the web.

- **Performance**: Flutter for Web compiles to high-performance JavaScript, ensuring that your app runs smoothly in the browser.
- **Hot Reload**: Just like in mobile development, Flutter for Web supports hot reload, enabling fast development and testing.

Setting Up a Flutter Web Project

Setting up a Flutter Web project is simple and follows the same setup process as creating a Flutter mobile app. However, you need to make sure that you have the correct environment configured for web development.

Steps to Set Up Flutter for Web:

1. **Ensure Flutter is Installed**: Make sure you have Flutter installed on your system. To check if Flutter supports web development, run:

   ```
   bash

   flutter doctor
   ```

   If web support is enabled, you should see `Chrome` listed under connected devices. If not, you can enable it with:

   ```
   bash
   ```

```
flutter config --enable-web
```

2. **Create a Flutter Web Project**: Create a new Flutter project as you would for a mobile app:

```
bash

flutter create my_web_app
```

Navigate to your project directory:

```
bash

cd my_web_app
```

3. **Run the Web App**: To run the app in the browser, use the following command:

```
bash

flutter run -d chrome
```

This will launch your Flutter app in a new Chrome browser window.

4. **Build the Web App**: Once you've finished developing your web app, you can build the production-ready version using:

bash

```
flutter build web
```

This will generate the build files in the `build/web` directory, which you can deploy to a web server.

Building Responsive Web UIs

Creating a responsive web UI is essential to ensure that your Flutter web app adapts to different screen sizes and resolutions. Flutter provides several tools and techniques to build responsive layouts that work seamlessly across devices.

Key Techniques for Building Responsive Web UIs:

1. **MediaQuery**: Use `MediaQuery` to get information about the device's screen size, orientation, and other properties. This can help you adjust the layout dynamically based on the screen dimensions.

   Example:

   dart

   ```
   MediaQuery.of(context).size.width
   ```

This will return the width of the screen, which you can use to make decisions about the layout.

2. **LayoutBuilder**: The `LayoutBuilder` widget gives you the constraints passed by the parent widget, allowing you to adjust your layout dynamically based on those constraints.

   Example:

```
dart

LayoutBuilder(
  builder: (context, constraints) {
    if (constraints.maxWidth > 600) {
      return Row(
        children: [/* Wide layout widgets
*/],
      );
    } else {
      return Column(
        children:    [/*    Narrow    layout
widgets */],
      );
    }
  },
)
```

This will build different layouts depending on the width of the container.

3. **Flexible and Expanded Widgets**: Use the `Flexible` and `Expanded` widgets to create flexible layouts that adjust based on the available space.

   Example:

```
dart


Row(
  children: <Widget>[
    Expanded(child:        Container(color:
Colors.red)),
    Expanded(child:        Container(color:
Colors.blue)),
  ],
)
```

   This will create two containers that take up equal space within a `Row`.

Flutter for Desktop: macOS, Windows, Linux

In addition to web development, Flutter now supports building desktop applications for macOS, Windows, and Linux. This allows developers to use Flutter's rich UI components and performance optimizations to build native desktop apps with a single codebase.

Setting Up Flutter for Desktop:

1. **Enable Desktop Support**: Desktop support is in the stable channel for macOS, Windows, and Linux. To enable desktop support, run:

   ```
   bash

   flutter config --enable-macos
   flutter config --enable-windows
   flutter config --enable-linux
   ```

2. **Create a Flutter Desktop Project**: To create a new Flutter project with desktop support, simply create a project as you would for mobile:

   ```
   bash

   flutter create my_desktop_app
   ```

   This will create a project that includes desktop platform directories (`macos`, `windows`, `linux`).

3. **Run the Desktop App**: To run the app on macOS, Windows, or Linux, use:

```bash
flutter run -d macos   # For macOS
flutter run -d windows # For Windows
flutter run -d linux   # For Linux
```

4. **Building the Desktop App**: Once the app is ready, you can build it for desktop with:

```bash
flutter build macos
flutter build windows
flutter build linux
```

This will generate the executable files for the corresponding platforms.

Real-World Example: Building a Cross-Platform App for Web and Desktop

Let's build a simple cross-platform Flutter app that works for both web and desktop. The app will have a button that changes the background color when clicked.

Step 1: Create a New Flutter Project

Create a new Flutter project using the following command:

```bash
flutter create cross_platform_app
```

Step 2: Modify the UI for Web and Desktop

In the `lib/main.dart` file, modify the UI to include a button that changes the background color:

```dart
import 'package:flutter/material.dart';

void main() {
  runApp(MyApp());
}

class MyApp extends StatefulWidget {
  @override
  _MyAppState createState() => _MyAppState();
}

class _MyAppState extends State<MyApp> {
  Color _backgroundColor = Colors.white;

  void _changeColor() {
    setState(() {
```

```
      _backgroundColor = _backgroundColor ==
Colors.white ? Colors.blue : Colors.white;
    });
  }

  @override
  Widget build(BuildContext context) {
    return MaterialApp(
      home: Scaffold(
        appBar: AppBar(title: Text('Cross-
Platform App')),
        body: Container(
          color: _backgroundColor,
          child: Center(
            child: ElevatedButton(
              onPressed: _changeColor,
              child: Text('Change Background
Color'),
            ),
          ),
        ),
      ),
    );
  }
}
```

Step 3: Make the App Responsive

Modify the UI to be responsive by using `LayoutBuilder` to adjust the layout based on the available screen size:

```
dart

LayoutBuilder(
  builder: (context, constraints) {
    if (constraints.maxWidth > 600) {
      return Row(
        children: [
          Expanded(child:        Container(color:
_backgroundColor)),
          Expanded(child:        Container(color:
_backgroundColor)),
        ],
      );
    } else {
      return Column(
        children: [
          Expanded(child:        Container(color:
_backgroundColor)),
          Expanded(child:        Container(color:
_backgroundColor)),
        ],
      );
    }
  },
)
```

Step 4: Run on Multiple Platforms

Now you can test the app across different platforms:

1. **Web**: Run the app in a browser:

   ```
   bash

   flutter run -d chrome
   ```

2. **macOS**: Run the app on macOS:

   ```
   bash

   flutter run -d macos
   ```

3. **Windows**: Run the app on Windows:

   ```
   bash

   flutter run -d windows
   ```

Step 5: Build for Multiple Platforms

To build the app for web and desktop:

1. **Web**:

   ```
   bash
   ```

```
flutter build web
```

2. **macOS**:

```bash
flutter build macos
```

3. **Windows**:

```bash
flutter build windows
```

Conclusion

In this chapter, we explored how to build apps with Flutter for multiple platforms, including web and desktop. We set up Flutter for web development, created responsive web UIs, and learned how to develop cross-platform desktop apps for macOS, Windows, and Linux. By following the steps and examples provided, you can create Flutter applications that run seamlessly across mobile, web, and desktop platforms with a single codebase. Flutter's ability to target multiple platforms makes it a powerful tool for building cross-platform apps, and in the next chapter, we will explore how to manage app state and improve performance in large Flutter applications.

CHAPTER 20

INTEGRATING WITH THIRD-PARTY SERVICES

Using REST APIs for External Data

Integrating third-party services into your Flutter app often involves making network requests to fetch external data. **REST APIs** (Representational State Transfer) are the most common method for interacting with external data sources in modern applications.

Making REST API Calls in Flutter:

Flutter provides the `http` package to facilitate making REST API calls. The `http` package allows you to send GET, POST, PUT, DELETE, and other HTTP requests, making it simple to interact with REST APIs.

Steps to Use REST APIs in Flutter:

1. **Add the `http` package to your `pubspec.yaml` file**:

   yaml

```
dependencies:
  flutter:
    sdk: flutter
  http: ^0.13.3
```

Run the command:

```
bash

flutter pub get
```

2. **Making a GET Request**: You can use the `http.get()` method to make a GET request and retrieve data from an API.

Example: Fetching data from a REST API:

```
dart

import 'package:http/http.dart' as http;
import 'dart:convert';

Future<void> fetchData() async {
  final          response          =          await
http.get(Uri.parse('https://jsonplacehold
er.typicode.com/posts'));

  if (response.statusCode == 200) {
```

```
    // If the server returns a 200 OK
response, parse the data
    List data =
json.decode(response.body);
    print(data); // Print the fetched data
  } else {
    throw Exception('Failed to load
data');
  }
}
```

3. **Handling JSON Data**: Often, the response data is in JSON format. You can use the `json.decode()` method from the `dart:convert` library to parse it into a Dart object.

Example: Parsing JSON into a Dart object:

```
dart

class Post {
  final int id;
  final String title;
  final String body;

  Post({required this.id, required
this.title, required this.body});
```

```
  factory        Post.fromJson(Map<String,
dynamic> json) {
    return Post(
      id: json['id'],
      title: json['title'],
      body: json['body'],
    );
  }
}

Future<void> fetchPosts() async {
  final       response        =       await
http.get(Uri.parse('https://jsonplacehold
er.typicode.com/posts'));

  if (response.statusCode == 200) {
    List              jsonResponse            =
json.decode(response.body);
    List<Post>             posts             =
jsonResponse.map((data)                     =>
Post.fromJson(data)).toList();
    print(posts);
  } else {
    throw   Exception('Failed   to   load
posts');
  }
}
```

Integrating Payment Gateways

Many apps require payment processing to handle transactions. Flutter supports integrating with payment gateways such as **Stripe**, **PayPal**, and **Razorpay** through third-party plugins.

Steps to Integrate Payment Gateways in Flutter:

1. **Integrating Stripe**: Stripe is one of the most popular payment gateways for mobile apps. To integrate Stripe in Flutter, you can use the `flutter_stripe` package.
   - **Add the `flutter_stripe` package**:

     yaml

     ```
     dependencies:
       flutter:
         sdk: flutter
       flutter_stripe: ^2.0.0
     ```

   - **Set up Stripe**: Follow the Stripe documentation to get your API keys and set up the Stripe configuration in your Flutter app.

   Example of creating a payment method:

   dart

```
import
'package:flutter_stripe/flutter_stripe.da
rt';

Future<void> createPaymentMethod() async {
  try {
    final    paymentMethod    =    await
Stripe.instance.createPaymentMethod(
      PaymentMethodParams.card(
        paymentMethodData:
PaymentMethodData(
          billingDetails:
BillingDetails(name: 'John Doe'),
        ),
      ),
    );
    print('Payment    Method    created:
${paymentMethod.id}');
  } catch (e) {
    print('Error: $e');
  }
}
```

This example demonstrates how to create a payment method using Stripe.

2. **Integrating PayPal**: PayPal also offers SDKs to handle payments in your app. You can integrate PayPal in Flutter using plugins like `flutter_paypal`.

Example:

```
dart

import
'package:flutter_paypal/flutter_paypal.da
rt';

void openPaypal() {
  FlutterPaypal.checkout(
    clientId: 'YOUR_PAYPAL_CLIENT_ID',
    secretKey: 'YOUR_PAYPAL_SECRET_KEY',
    currency: 'USD',
    amount: '10.00',
    onSuccess: (response) {
      print('Payment Success: $response');
    },
    onError: (error) {
      print('Payment Error: $error');
    },
  );
}
```

This example demonstrates a simple PayPal checkout process. You need to replace the `YOUR_PAYPAL_CLIENT_ID` and `YOUR_PAYPAL_SECRET_KEY` with your actual PayPal credentials.

Working with Analytics Services like Firebase Analytics

Analytics helps you understand how users interact with your app. **Firebase Analytics** is a robust solution for collecting and analyzing app usage data, tracking events, and monitoring user behavior.

Steps to Integrate Firebase Analytics:

1. **Add Firebase Analytics to Your Project**: First, add the `firebase_analytics` package to your `pubspec.yaml` file:

   ```
   yaml

   dependencies:
     firebase_analytics: ^9.0.0
   ```

2. **Initialize Firebase Analytics**: You need to initialize Firebase in your app. Make sure Firebase is initialized in the `main.dart` file:

   ```
   dart

   import
   'package:firebase_core/firebase_core.dart
   ';
   ```

```
import 'package:flutter/material.dart';

void main() async {

WidgetsFlutterBinding.ensureInitialized()
;
  await Firebase.initializeApp();
  runApp(MyApp());
}
```

3. **Log Events in Firebase Analytics**: Once Firebase Analytics is set up, you can log custom events and track user interactions.

   Example:

```
dart

import
'package:firebase_analytics/firebase_anal
ytics.dart';

class AnalyticsService {
  final FirebaseAnalytics _analytics =
FirebaseAnalytics();

  Future<void> logEvent(String eventName,
Map<String, dynamic> parameters) async {
    await _analytics.logEvent(
      name: eventName,
```

```
        parameters: parameters,
      );
    }
  }

  // Example usage
  AnalyticsService().logEvent('item_purchas
  ed', {'item_id': '1234', 'price': 9.99});
```

In this example, we log an event named `item_purchased` with additional parameters like the `item_id` and `price`.

4. **View Analytics Data**: Once events are logged, you can view analytics data in the Firebase Console under the **Analytics** section. Firebase will provide insights into user behaviors, such as app usage, purchase activities, and retention rates.

Real-World Example: Adding Payment Integration to an App

Let's walk through adding **Stripe** payment integration to a Flutter app. We will create a simple payment flow where users can make a payment using their credit card.

Step 1: Set Up Stripe:

First, sign up for a Stripe account and retrieve your **API keys** from the Stripe Dashboard.

Step 2: Add Stripe Dependencies:

Add `flutter_stripe` to your `pubspec.yaml`:

```
yaml

dependencies:
  flutter_stripe: ^2.0.0
```

Step 3: Initialize Stripe:

In your `main.dart`, initialize Stripe with your API keys:

```
dart

import
'package:flutter_stripe/flutter_stripe.dart';

void main() async {
  WidgetsFlutterBinding.ensureInitialized();
  await Stripe.instance.applySettings(
    appleMerchantIdentifier:
'merchant.com.yourapp',
    stripePublishableKey:
'YOUR_STRIPE_PUBLISHABLE_KEY',
```

```
    androidPayMode:   'test',   //   Change   to
'production' for production
  );
  runApp(MyApp());
}
```

Step 4: Implement Payment Flow:

Create a simple UI with a button that initiates the payment process.

```
dart

import 'package:flutter/material.dart';
import
'package:flutter_stripe/flutter_stripe.dart';

class PaymentScreen extends StatelessWidget {
  Future<void> handlePayment() async {
    try {
      // Create a Payment Intent on your backend
      final  paymentIntentClientSecret  =  await
createPaymentIntent();

      // Confirm the payment using Stripe
      await Stripe.instance.confirmPayment(
        paymentIntentClientSecret,
        PaymentMethodParams.card(),
      );
```

```
    } catch (e) {
      print('Error: $e');
    }
  }

  @override
  Widget build(BuildContext context) {
    return Scaffold(
      appBar:     AppBar(title:     Text('Stripe
Payment')),
      body: Center(
        child: ElevatedButton(
          onPressed: handlePayment,
          child: Text('Pay with Stripe'),
        ),
      ),
    );
  }
}
```

In this example:

- We call `createPaymentIntent()` to get the Payment Intent from your backend (this is where you would integrate with your server to create the payment intent).
- Then, we use `Stripe.instance.confirmPayment()` to confirm the payment.

Step 5: Backend Setup for Payment Intent:

On the server side, create a Payment Intent using your Stripe secret key:

```javascript
const stripe = require('stripe')('YOUR_STRIPE_SECRET_KEY');

app.post('/create-payment-intent', async (req, res) => {
  const paymentIntent = await stripe.paymentIntents.create({
    amount: 1000, // Amount in cents (e.g., $10.00)
    currency: 'usd',
  });

  res.send({
    clientSecret: paymentIntent.client_secret,
  });
});
```

Conclusion

In this chapter, we learned how to integrate **REST APIs** for external data, **payment gateways** like **Stripe**, and **analytics services** such as **Firebase Analytics** into our Flutter app. We also walked through the process of adding **Stripe payment**

integration to a Flutter app, providing a real-world example of how to process payments. Integrating third-party services like APIs, payments, and analytics is essential for building feature-rich apps, and with the steps covered in this chapter, you can now add these powerful services to your Flutter applications. In the next chapter, we will explore further optimizations and strategies for building scalable Flutter apps.

CHAPTER 21

USING ADVANCED FLUTTER WIDGETS

Custom Widgets in Flutter

Widgets are the building blocks of a Flutter app's UI. Flutter provides a wide range of pre-built widgets, but one of its most powerful features is the ability to create **custom widgets**. Custom widgets allow you to design reusable components tailored to the specific needs of your app.

Why Create Custom Widgets?

- **Reusability**: Custom widgets can be reused across your app, making your code cleaner and easier to maintain.
- **Encapsulation**: Custom widgets allow you to encapsulate logic and UI into self-contained units, making the code easier to understand and debug.
- **Tailored Design**: With custom widgets, you can create complex UIs that go beyond the basic Flutter widgets, implementing unique designs and behaviors.

Creating a Simple Custom Widget

Creating a custom widget in Flutter involves extending either `StatelessWidget` or `StatefulWidget`. The key difference between these two is that `StatefulWidget` can hold mutable state, while `StatelessWidget` is immutable.

Example of a custom widget:

```
dart

import 'package:flutter/material.dart';

class CustomCard extends StatelessWidget {
  final String title;
  final String content;

  CustomCard({required this.title, required
this.content});

  @override
  Widget build(BuildContext context) {
    return Card(
      elevation: 5,
      margin: EdgeInsets.all(16),
      child: Padding(
        padding: EdgeInsets.all(16),
        child: Column(
          crossAxisAlignment:
CrossAxisAlignment.start,
          children: [
```

```
            Text(title,                          style:
TextStyle(fontSize:        20,        fontWeight:
FontWeight.bold)),
            SizedBox(height: 8),
            Text(content),
          ],
        ),
      ),
    );
  }
}
```

In this example, `CustomCard` is a custom widget that takes a `title` and `content` as parameters and displays them in a card with some styling. You can reuse this widget throughout your app to display cards with different titles and contents.

Building Complex Widgets with StatefulWidget

Sometimes, you need a widget that changes over time based on user interaction or external events. For this, you would use a `StatefulWidget`, which allows you to maintain mutable state that can be updated dynamically.

StatefulWidget Basics

- **StatefulWidget**: This is a widget that has a mutable state. It requires two classes: one for the widget itself (the `StatefulWidget` class) and one for the state (the `State` class).
- **State**: The state class holds the mutable data for the widget and manages its lifecycle.

Example: A Counter Widget

Here's a simple example of a counter widget that increments the count when a button is pressed:

```
dart

import 'package:flutter/material.dart';

class CounterWidget extends StatefulWidget {
  @override
  _CounterWidgetState createState() =>
_CounterWidgetState();
}

class _CounterWidgetState extends
State<CounterWidget> {
  int _counter = 0;

  void _incrementCounter() {
    setState(() {
      _counter++;
```

```
    });
  }

  @override
  Widget build(BuildContext context) {
    return Column(
      mainAxisAlignment:
MainAxisAlignment.center,
      children: [
        Text('Counter:    $_counter',    style:
TextStyle(fontSize: 24)),
        ElevatedButton(
          onPressed: _incrementCounter,
          child: Text('Increment'),
        ),
      ],
    );
  }
}
```

In this example:

- `CounterWidget` is a `StatefulWidget`.
- `_CounterWidgetState` holds the mutable state (the counter) and defines the logic to increment the counter when the button is pressed.
- `setState()` is used to update the widget's state, which triggers a rebuild of the widget.

StatefulWidget Lifecycle

The lifecycle of a `StatefulWidget` consists of:

1. **`createState()`**: Called when the widget is inserted into the widget tree.
2. **`initState()`**: Called when the state object is created.
3. **`build()`**: Called every time the widget needs to be redrawn.
4. **`dispose()`**: Called when the widget is removed from the widget tree, where you should clean up resources like listeners.

Leveraging Flutter's CustomPainter for Graphics

Sometimes, you may need to draw custom graphics or animations directly within your app, such as charts, diagrams, or custom progress indicators. Flutter provides the `CustomPainter` class, which allows you to create custom drawings by overriding the `paint()` method.

Using CustomPainter

The `CustomPainter` class lets you draw shapes, lines, text, and other custom graphics directly onto a `Canvas`. You can control the appearance and position of your graphics using the drawing methods available in the `Canvas` class.

Example: Drawing a Circle

Here's an example of how to draw a simple circle using `CustomPainter`:

```
dart

import 'package:flutter/material.dart';

class CirclePainter extends CustomPainter {
  @override
  void paint(Canvas canvas, Size size) {
    Paint paint = Paint()
      ..color = Colors.blue
      ..style = PaintingStyle.fill;

    canvas.drawCircle(Offset(size.width / 2,
size.height / 2), 50, paint);
  }

  @override
  bool shouldRepaint(CustomPainter oldDelegate)
{
    return false; // No need to repaint unless
the data changes
  }
```

```
}

class CircleWidget extends StatelessWidget {
  @override
  Widget build(BuildContext context) {
    return CustomPaint(
      size: Size(200, 200), // Set size of the
custom painting area
      painter: CirclePainter(),
    );
  }
}
```

In this example:

- The `CirclePainter` class is a custom painter that draws a blue circle in the center of the canvas.
- `CustomPaint` is a widget that uses the `CirclePainter` to render the circle on the screen.

CustomPainter Use Cases

You can use `CustomPainter` to create more complex drawings, such as:

- **Custom charts and graphs** (e.g., bar charts, line graphs).
- **Games** or interactive graphics.
- **Custom progress indicators** (e.g., circular or linear progress bars).

Real-World Example: Creating a Custom Circular Progress Indicator

Let's build a custom circular progress indicator using `CustomPainter`. This example will allow you to display a progress value (from 0 to 100) in a circular form.

Step 1: Define the CustomPainter

We'll create a custom painter that draws a circular progress indicator.

```
dart

class CircularProgressPainter extends
CustomPainter {
  final double progress;

  CircularProgressPainter(this.progress);

  @override
  void paint(Canvas canvas, Size size) {
    Paint paint = Paint()
      ..color = Colors.grey
      ..style = PaintingStyle.stroke
      ..strokeWidth = 10;
```

```
    // Draw the background circle
    canvas.drawCircle(Offset(size.width / 2,
size.height / 2), size.width / 2, paint);

    // Draw the progress arc
    paint.color = Colors.blue;
    paint.strokeCap = StrokeCap.round;
    canvas.drawArc(
      Rect.fromCircle(center: Offset(size.width
/ 2, size.height / 2), radius: size.width / 2),
      -1.57, // Starting angle (top of the
circle)
      2 * 3.14 * (progress / 100), // Progress
angle based on percentage
      false,
      paint,
    );
  }

  @override
  bool shouldRepaint(CustomPainter oldDelegate)
{
    return false;
  }
}
```

In this `CircularProgressPainter`:

- The `paint()` method draws the background circle and the progress arc.
- The `progress` parameter is used to calculate the angle for the progress arc based on the percentage (0 to 100).

Step 2: Use CustomPainter in a Widget

Now, let's use this custom painter in a widget that updates the progress dynamically.

```
dart

class CircularProgressWidget extends
StatefulWidget {
  @override
  _CircularProgressWidgetState createState() =>
_CircularProgressWidgetState();
}

class _CircularProgressWidgetState extends
State<CircularProgressWidget> {
  double _progress = 0;

  void _updateProgress() {
    setState(() {
      _progress = (_progress + 10) % 110; //
Increment progress
    });
  }
```

```
  @override
  Widget build(BuildContext context) {
    return Scaffold(
      appBar:     AppBar(title:     Text('Custom
Circular Progress Indicator')),
      body: Center(
        child: Column(
          mainAxisAlignment:
MainAxisAlignment.center,
          children: [
            CustomPaint(
              size: Size(200, 200),
              painter:
CircularProgressPainter(_progress),
            ),
            SizedBox(height: 20),
            ElevatedButton(
              onPressed: _updateProgress,
              child: Text('Update Progress'),
            ),
          ],
        ),
      ),
    );
  }
}
```

Explanation:

- The `CircularProgressWidget` is a `StatefulWidget` that updates the progress when the button is pressed.
- The `CustomPaint` widget uses the `CircularProgressPainter` to draw the circular progress indicator on the screen.
- The progress value (`_progress`) is updated on each button press, and the arc is redrawn with the new progress value.

Conclusion

In this chapter, we explored advanced Flutter widgets, including custom widgets, stateful widgets, and the use of `CustomPainter` for drawing graphics. We learned how to create custom widgets, build complex UI components with `StatefulWidget`, and use `CustomPainter` to create custom graphics such as progress indicators. Through the real-world example of creating a custom circular progress indicator, we demonstrated how to combine these techniques to build dynamic, interactive UIs in Flutter. In the next chapter, we will delve into further advanced topics such as handling background tasks and creating custom plugins in Flutter.

CHAPTER 22

ADVANCED STATE MANAGEMENT SOLUTIONS

Deep Dive into Provider and Riverpod

State management is one of the most crucial aspects of building scalable and maintainable Flutter apps. In this chapter, we'll explore some advanced state management solutions that help manage and maintain the app state efficiently: **Provider**, **Riverpod**, **BLoC**, and **Redux**.

Provider: The Flutter State Management Library

Provider is one of the most popular state management libraries in Flutter, providing a simple and efficient way to manage app state. It works on the principle of **dependency injection**, where you can expose objects to widgets in a way that they can be accessed and modified without directly passing data.

How Provider Works

Provider allows you to inject objects into the widget tree and listen for changes. It's lightweight, easy to use, and works well with both simple and complex state management scenarios.

1. **Setting Up Provider**: First, you need to add the `provider` dependency to your `pubspec.yaml` file:

   ```
   yaml

   dependencies:
     flutter:
       sdk: flutter
     provider: ^6.0.1
   ```

2. **Creating a Simple State with Provider**: Here's an example of how to use Provider to manage a simple counter state:

   ```
   dart

   import 'package:flutter/material.dart';
   import 'package:provider/provider.dart';

   void main() {
     runApp(MyApp());
   }
   ```

```
class Counter with ChangeNotifier {
  int _count = 0;

  int get count => _count;

  void increment() {
    _count++;
    notifyListeners();
  }
}

class MyApp extends StatelessWidget {
  @override
  Widget build(BuildContext context) {
    return ChangeNotifierProvider(
      create: (context) => Counter(),
      child: MaterialApp(
        home: HomeScreen(),
      ),
    );
  }
}

class HomeScreen extends StatelessWidget {
  @override
  Widget build(BuildContext context) {
    final            counter            =
Provider.of<Counter>(context);
```

```
    return Scaffold(
      appBar: AppBar(title: Text('Provider
Example')),
      body: Center(
        child: Column(
          mainAxisAlignment:
MainAxisAlignment.center,
          children: <Widget>[
            Text('Counter:
${counter.count}',                    style:
TextStyle(fontSize: 24)),
            ElevatedButton(
              onPressed:
counter.increment,
              child: Text('Increment'),
            ),
          ],
        ),
      ),
    );
  }
}
```

In this example:

- The `Counter` class is a `ChangeNotifier` that holds the counter value and notifies listeners when the value changes.

- `ChangeNotifierProvider` provides the `Counter` object to the widget tree, allowing widgets like `HomeScreen` to access and listen for changes in the counter state.
- When the `increment` method is called, the `notifyListeners()` method triggers a rebuild of the widgets that depend on the state.

Riverpod: A More Robust Provider Alternative

Riverpod is a more advanced state management solution from the same creator as Provider. It builds on Provider's concepts but introduces a more powerful, testable, and flexible approach to state management. Riverpod removes many of the limitations of Provider, such as relying on `BuildContext` to access state.

1. **Setting Up Riverpod**: First, add the `flutter_riverpod` dependency to your `pubspec.yaml`:

   yaml

   ```
   dependencies:
     flutter:
       sdk: flutter
     flutter_riverpod: ^1.0.0
   ```

2. **Creating a Simple State with Riverpod**: Here's how you can manage the counter state using Riverpod:

```
dart

import 'package:flutter/material.dart';
import
'package:flutter_riverpod/flutter_riverpo
d.dart';

void main() {
  runApp(ProviderScope(child: MyApp()));
}

final              counterProvider              =
StateProvider<int>((ref) => 0);

class MyApp extends StatelessWidget {
  @override
  Widget build(BuildContext context) {
    return MaterialApp(
      home: HomeScreen(),
    );
  }
}

class HomeScreen extends ConsumerWidget {
  @override
```

```
  Widget    build(BuildContext    context,
WidgetRef ref) {
    final            counter            =
ref.watch(counterProvider);

    return Scaffold(
      appBar: AppBar(title: Text('Riverpod
Example')),
      body: Center(
        child: Column(
          mainAxisAlignment:
MainAxisAlignment.center,
          children: <Widget>[
            Text('Counter:      $counter',
style: TextStyle(fontSize: 24)),
            ElevatedButton(
              onPressed:       ()        =>
ref.read(counterProvider.notifier).state+
+,
              child: Text('Increment'),
            ),
          ],
        ),
      ),
    );
  }
}
```

In this example:

- `counterProvider` is a `StateProvider` that manages the state of the counter.
- The `ConsumerWidget` allows us to access and rebuild the widget when the state changes.
- `ref.watch(counterProvider)` listens for changes in the counter state and updates the UI accordingly.
- To modify the state, we use `ref.read(counterProvider.notifier).state++`.

BLoC (Business Logic Component) Architecture

BLoC is an architectural pattern for managing app state by separating business logic from UI code. It is a reactive programming model that uses **Streams** to manage and pass data between the UI and business logic.

How BLoC Works:

1. **BLoC**: Contains the business logic and exposes streams of data.
2. **Events**: Represent user actions or other triggers.
3. **States**: Represent the app's UI state.

BLoC listens for events and emits states to the UI. The UI listens for state changes and updates accordingly.

Setting Up BLoC:

1. **Add the BLoC dependencies**:

   ```
   yaml

   dependencies:
     flutter_bloc: ^8.0.1
   ```

2. **Creating a BLoC Example**:

   Example of a simple BLoC pattern to manage a counter:

   ```
   dart

   import 'package:flutter/material.dart';
   import
   'package:flutter_bloc/flutter_bloc.dart';

   // Counter Events
   abstract class CounterEvent {}

   class IncrementEvent extends CounterEvent
   {}

   // Counter State
   class CounterState {
     final int counter;
     CounterState(this.counter);
   }
   ```

```
// Counter BLoC
class             CounterBloc            extends
Bloc<CounterEvent, CounterState> {
  CounterBloc() : super(CounterState(0));

  @override
  Stream<CounterState>
mapEventToState(CounterEvent event) async*
{
    if (event is IncrementEvent) {
      yield  CounterState(state.counter  +
1);
    }
  }
}

void main() {
  runApp(MyApp());
}

class MyApp extends StatelessWidget {
  @override
  Widget build(BuildContext context) {
    return BlocProvider(
      create: (context) => CounterBloc(),
      child: MaterialApp(
        home: HomeScreen(),
      ),
```

```
    );
  }
}

class HomeScreen extends StatelessWidget {
  @override
  Widget build(BuildContext context) {
    return Scaffold(
      appBar:   AppBar(title:   Text('BLoC
Example')),
      body: Center(
        child: Column(
          mainAxisAlignment:
MainAxisAlignment.center,
          children: <Widget>[
            BlocBuilder<CounterBloc,
CounterState>(
              builder: (context, state) {
                return      Text('Counter:
${state.counter}',                  style:
TextStyle(fontSize: 24));
              },
            ),
            ElevatedButton(
              onPressed: () {

context.read<CounterBloc>().add(Increment
Event());
              },
```

```
                    child: Text('Increment'),
                  ),
                ],
              ),
            ),
          );
        }
      }
```

In this example:

- CounterBloc listens for IncrementEvent and emits a new state with an incremented counter value.
- BlocProvider provides the CounterBloc to the widget tree.
- BlocBuilder listens for state changes and rebuilds the UI when the counter changes.

Using Redux for App State Management

Redux is another popular state management solution, inspired by the Redux pattern from JavaScript. It works by maintaining a single global state object and dispatching actions to modify the state.

How Redux Works:

1. **State**: A single, immutable global state object.
2. **Actions**: Objects that represent events that modify the state.
3. **Reducers**: Functions that handle actions and update the state.

Setting Up Redux:

1. **Add the Redux dependencies**:

```
yaml

dependencies:
  flutter_redux: ^0.7.0
  redux: ^5.0.0
```

2. **Creating a Redux Example**:

Example of a Redux pattern to manage a counter:

```
dart

import 'package:flutter/material.dart';
import
'package:flutter_redux/flutter_redux.dart
';
import 'package:redux/redux.dart';

// App State
```

```
class AppState {
  final int counter;
  AppState(this.counter);
}

// Actions
class IncrementAction {}

// Reducer
AppState  counterReducer(AppState  state,
dynamic action) {
  if (action is IncrementAction) {
    return AppState(state.counter + 1);
  }
  return state;
}

void main() {
  final store = Store<AppState>(
    counterReducer,
    initialState: AppState(0),
  );

  runApp(MyApp(store: store));
}

class MyApp extends StatelessWidget {
  final Store<AppState> store;
  MyApp({required this.store});
```

```
  @override
  Widget build(BuildContext context) {
    return StoreProvider(
      store: store,
      child: MaterialApp(
        home: HomeScreen(),
      ),
    );
  }
}

class HomeScreen extends StatelessWidget {
  @override
  Widget build(BuildContext context) {
    return Scaffold(
      appBar:  AppBar(title:  Text('Redux
Example')),
      body: Center(
        child: Column(
          mainAxisAlignment:
MainAxisAlignment.center,
          children: <Widget>[
            StoreConnector<AppState, int>(
              converter:    (store)    =>
store.state.counter,
              builder: (context, counter)
{
```

```
                return       Text('Counter:
$counter',    style:    TextStyle(fontSize:
24));
              },
            ),
            ElevatedButton(
              onPressed: () {

StoreProvider.of<AppState>(context).dispa
tch(IncrementAction());
              },
              child: Text('Increment'),
            ),
          ],
        ),
      ),
    );
  }
}
```

In this example:

- We define the `AppState` as a simple class with a counter.
- `IncrementAction` is the action that triggers a state update.
- The `counterReducer` function updates the state when an `IncrementAction` is dispatched.
- The `Store` holds the state and dispatches actions.

Real-World Example: Managing Complex App State with BLoC

In a real-world scenario, you might need to manage complex state across multiple screens and user actions. Using the **BLoC** pattern is ideal for this kind of task.

Imagine building an app where users can create, edit, and delete tasks. Each task has a title, description, and completion status.

1. **Define Task Events**:
   - Add, update, or delete tasks.
2. **Define Task States**:
   - Task List Loaded, Task Added, Task Deleted.
3. **Implement BLoC Logic**:
   - Map events to states and update the UI based on changes.

Conclusion

In this chapter, we explored advanced state management solutions in Flutter, including **Provider**, **Riverpod**, **BLoC**, and **Redux**. We covered the fundamentals of each state management pattern, highlighted their use cases, and demonstrated how to manage complex app state. By understanding these patterns, you can choose the best approach for your app based on complexity, scalability, and maintainability. In the next chapter, we will dive into performance optimization techniques and best practices for large-scale Flutter applications.

CHAPTER 23

ADVANCED ANIMATIONS IN FLUTTER

Creating Complex Animations with AnimationController

Animations are an essential part of creating engaging and dynamic user experiences. Flutter provides a powerful animation framework that allows you to create complex animations using `AnimationController`, `Tween`, and `AnimatedBuilder`.

The `AnimationController` is responsible for controlling the animation's duration, starting and stopping the animation, and controlling the animation's progress over time.

Key Concepts:

1. **AnimationController**: Manages the animation's state, duration, and progress.
2. **Tween**: Specifies how the animation should transform values over time (e.g., from `0` to `1`, or from one color to another).

3. **AnimatedBuilder**: A widget that rebuilds the UI as the animation progresses, making it efficient for more complex animations.

Creating an Animation with AnimationController

1. **Setting up AnimationController**: To create an animation, you need to initialize an `AnimationController` and use it with a `Tween` to animate a value.

```
dart

import 'package:flutter/material.dart';

void main() {
  runApp(MyApp());
}

class MyApp extends StatelessWidget {
  @override
  Widget build(BuildContext context) {
    return MaterialApp(
      home: AnimatedContainerScreen(),
    );
  }
}
```

```
class        AnimatedContainerScreen        extends
StatefulWidget {
  @override
  _AnimatedContainerScreenState createState() =>
      _AnimatedContainerScreenState();
}

class    _AnimatedContainerScreenState    extends
State<AnimatedContainerScreen>
    with TickerProviderStateMixin {
  late AnimationController _controller;
  late Animation<double> _animation;

  @override
  void initState() {
    super.initState();
    _controller = AnimationController(
      duration: Duration(seconds: 2),
      vsync: this,
    );
    _animation  =  Tween<double>(begin:  0,  end:
200).animate(_controller)
      ..addListener(() {
        setState(() {});
      });
    _controller.repeat(reverse: true);
  }

  @override
```

```
  void dispose() {
    _controller.dispose();
    super.dispose();
  }

  @override
  Widget build(BuildContext context) {
    return Scaffold(
      appBar:    AppBar(title:    Text('Animated
Container')),
      body: Center(
        child: Container(
          width: _animation.value,
          height: _animation.value,
          color: Colors.blue,
        ),
      ),
    );
  }
}
```

Explanation:

- **AnimationController**: Manages the animation for 2 seconds and repeats with a reverse cycle.
- **Tween**: Specifies that the animation will start from `0` and end at `200`.

- **Animated Container**: The size of the container changes based on the `_animation` value, giving it a smooth animation effect.

Implicit and Custom Curves for Advanced Animations

In addition to controlling the animation's duration and values, you can further enhance the animation's smoothness and natural flow by customizing the **curves**.

Using Implicit Curves

Flutter provides several built-in **Implicit Curves** that define how the values of an animation change over time. These curves can make animations feel more natural and less mechanical.

Common built-in curves:

1. **Curves.easeIn**: Starts slow and speeds up towards the end.
2. **Curves.easeOut**: Starts fast and slows down towards the end.
3. **Curves.easeInOut**: Starts slow, speeds up, and slows down again.
4. **Curves.elasticIn**: Starts slow, then moves in an oscillating motion before slowing down.

Example of using `easeInOut`:

```
dart

_controller = AnimationController(
  duration: Duration(seconds: 2),
  vsync: this,
);

_animation = Tween<double>(begin: 0, end: 200)
    .animate(CurvedAnimation(parent:
_controller, curve: Curves.easeInOut));
```

Creating Custom Curves

If the built-in curves don't suit your needs, you can create custom curves by defining a `Curve` object. Custom curves allow you to fine-tune the animation timing to match your desired effect.

Example of creating a custom curve:

```
dart

class MyCustomCurve extends Curve {
  @override
  double transform(double t) {
    return t * t; // Quadratic curve
  }
}
```

```
_animation = Tween<double>(begin: 0, end: 200)
    .animate(CurvedAnimation(parent:
_controller, curve: MyCustomCurve()));
```

Explanation of Custom Curves:

- In the `MyCustomCurve`, the `transform()` method defines the custom interpolation function for the animation. The curve here is quadratic, so the animation starts slow and accelerates as it progresses.

Transitioning Between Screens with Animations

Flutter allows you to animate the transition between screens, giving your app a polished, professional feel. You can animate screen transitions using **PageRouteBuilder** or by using pre-built widgets such as **AnimatedSwitcher**.

Using PageRouteBuilder for Custom Screen Transitions

`PageRouteBuilder` allows you to create custom animations when transitioning between screens.

Example:

```
dart

Navigator.of(context).push(PageRouteBuilder(
  pageBuilder: (context, animation, secondaryAnimation) => NewScreen(),
  transitionsBuilder: (context, animation, secondaryAnimation, child) {
    const begin = Offset(1.0, 0.0);
    const end = Offset.zero;
    const curve = Curves.easeInOut;

    var tween = Tween(begin: begin, end: end).chain(CurveTween(curve: curve));
    var offsetAnimation = animation.drive(tween);

    return SlideTransition(position: offsetAnimation, child: child);
  },
));
```

In this example:

- **PageRouteBuilder** is used to create a custom route.
- **SlideTransition** animates the new screen sliding in from the right.
- **Tween** defines the start and end positions for the animation.

Using AnimatedSwitcher for UI Element Transitions

If you want to animate the transition of individual widgets within a screen, you can use `AnimatedSwitcher`, which smoothly transitions between two widgets.

```
dart

AnimatedSwitcher(
  duration: Duration(seconds: 1),
  child: _isFirst ? FirstWidget() : SecondWidget(),
)
```

Here, `AnimatedSwitcher` animates the transition between `FirstWidget` and `SecondWidget` when `_isFirst` changes. You can use different transitions such as fade, scale, or slide.

Real-World Example: Creating a Complex UI Animation for a Profile Screen

In this real-world example, let's create an animated profile screen where the profile image and text smoothly transition as the user taps a button to toggle between "Edit" and "View" modes.

Step 1: Define the Profile Screen Layout

We'll create a `StatefulWidget` with a profile picture and text. When the user clicks a button, we will animate the transition between the profile image and an editable text field.

```
dart

import 'package:flutter/material.dart';

class ProfileScreen extends StatefulWidget {
  @override
  _ProfileScreenState createState() =>
_ProfileScreenState();
}

class _ProfileScreenState extends
State<ProfileScreen> with
TickerProviderStateMixin {
  late AnimationController _controller;
  bool _isEditing = false;

  @override
  void initState() {
    super.initState();
    _controller = AnimationController(
      duration: Duration(seconds: 1),
      vsync: this,
    );
```

```
  }

  @override
  void dispose() {
    _controller.dispose();
    super.dispose();
  }

  void _toggleEditMode() {
    setState(() {
      _isEditing = !_isEditing;
    });
    if (_isEditing) {
      _controller.forward();
    } else {
      _controller.reverse();
    }
  }

  @override
  Widget build(BuildContext context) {
    return Scaffold(
      appBar: AppBar(title: Text('Profile')),
      body: Center(
        child: Column(
          mainAxisAlignment:
MainAxisAlignment.center,
          children: [
            AnimatedBuilder(
```

```
            animation: _controller,
            builder: (context, child) {
              return Transform.scale(
                scale: _controller.value,
                child: child,
              );
            },
            child: CircleAvatar(
              radius: 50,
              backgroundImage:
NetworkImage('https://via.placeholder.com/150')
,
            ),
          ),
          SizedBox(height: 20),
          AnimatedSwitcher(
            duration: Duration(seconds: 1),
            child: _isEditing
                ? TextField(
                    key: ValueKey('edit'),
                    decoration:
InputDecoration(hintText: 'Edit Name'),
                  )
                : Text(
                    'John Doe',
                    key: ValueKey('view'),
                    style: TextStyle(fontSize:
24, fontWeight: FontWeight.bold),
                  ),
```

```
            ),
            SizedBox(height: 20),
            ElevatedButton(
              onPressed: _toggleEditMode,
              child: Text(_isEditing ? 'Save' :
'Edit'),
            ),
          ],
        ),
      ),
    );
  }
}
```

Step 2: Explanation

- **Profile Image Animation**: When the user taps the "Edit" button, we animate the profile image using `Transform.scale` inside an `AnimatedBuilder`. The scale value changes based on the `_controller`'s animation progress.
- **Text Transition**: We use `AnimatedSwitcher` to smoothly transition between the `TextField` (for editing) and the `Text` widget (for viewing the name). When `_isEditing` is `true`, the `TextField` is shown, and when it is `false`, the regular `Text` widget is shown.
- **Button Action**: The button toggles between editing and viewing mode. It uses `_controller.forward()` to

start the animation and `_controller.reverse()` to reverse it.

Conclusion

In this chapter, we explored advanced animations in Flutter, including how to create complex animations using `AnimationController`, leverage custom curves for advanced effects, and transition between screens with animations. We also created a real-world example of animating a profile screen with a smooth transition between edit and view modes. Flutter's animation framework is powerful, and with the techniques covered in this chapter, you can create rich, interactive, and dynamic user interfaces for your Flutter apps. In the next chapter, we will explore advanced app architectures and best practices for scaling your Flutter applications.

CHAPTER 24

SECURITY IN FLUTTER APPS

Securing User Data and Information

As developers, ensuring the security of user data is a fundamental responsibility. Flutter provides multiple tools and techniques to help protect sensitive data and secure communication between the app and backend services.

Why is Security Important in Flutter Apps?

With the rise of data breaches and cyberattacks, protecting sensitive data—such as user credentials, personal information, and payment details—is crucial. Security measures ensure that attackers can't exploit your app and access user data.

Key Security Considerations in Flutter Apps:

1. **Encryption**: Encrypting sensitive data ensures that even if an attacker gains access to the database or storage, they won't be able to read it.
2. **Authentication**: Ensuring that users are who they say they are (using tokens, passwords, etc.) and protecting sensitive user information.

3. **Secure Communication**: Use HTTPS to encrypt data during transmission and protect against man-in-the-middle (MITM) attacks.
4. **Data Storage**: Store sensitive data securely and follow best practices for encryption.

Implementing Secure Authentication (JWT, OAuth)

Authentication is the process of verifying a user's identity, and secure authentication methods are essential for protecting user data. In Flutter apps, you often need to integrate with authentication providers like **JWT (JSON Web Tokens)** or **OAuth** for secure login and user management.

JWT (JSON Web Token) Authentication

JWT is a compact, URL-safe means of representing claims to be transferred between two parties. It is often used for authenticating users by generating a token that includes the user's identity and is signed by a server. The client can then send this token in subsequent requests to prove its identity.

Steps to Implement JWT Authentication:

1. **User Logs In**: The user provides their credentials (e.g., username and password).

2. **Server Issues JWT**: After verifying the credentials, the server generates a JWT and sends it back to the client.
3. **Client Sends JWT in Future Requests**: The client sends the JWT in the Authorization header for every future API request. The server then verifies the token and grants access.

Example of JWT Authentication: Here's a simplified approach to handling JWT in Flutter:

```
dart

import 'package:flutter/material.dart';
import 'package:http/http.dart' as http;
import 'dart:convert';

class AuthService {
  final String apiUrl = 'https://example.com/api/login';

  Future<String?> login(String username, String password) async {
    final response = await http.post(
      Uri.parse(apiUrl),
      body: json.encode({'username': username, 'password': password}),
      headers: {'Content-Type': 'application/json'},
    );
```

```
    if (response.statusCode == 200) {
      var data = json.decode(response.body);
      return data['token'];  // JWT Token
    } else {
      throw Exception('Failed to login');
    }
  }
}
```

Using JWT in Requests:

Once the JWT is obtained, you can use it to authenticate requests to a secured API.

```
dart

Future<void> fetchData(String token) async {
  final response = await http.get(
    Uri.parse('https://example.com/protected-
data'),
    headers: {
      'Authorization': 'Bearer $token',
      'Content-Type': 'application/json'
    },
  );

  if (response.statusCode == 200) {
    print('Data: ${response.body}');
```

```
    } else {
      throw Exception('Failed to load data');
    }
}
```

OAuth Authentication

OAuth is a popular open-standard authorization protocol that allows third-party apps to access user data without exposing user credentials. OAuth is commonly used for integrating with services like Google, Facebook, and Twitter.

OAuth Flow:

1. **User Redirected to Authorization Server**: The app redirects the user to the OAuth provider's authorization page (e.g., Google login).
2. **User Grants Permissions**: The user grants permission for the app to access their data.
3. **Authorization Code**: The authorization server redirects the user back to the app with an authorization code.
4. **Exchange Code for Access Token**: The app exchanges the authorization code for an access token, which can be used to make authorized API calls.

OAuth with Google:

For OAuth-based authentication, you can use the `google_sign_in` package in Flutter to handle Google login.

1. **Add the Google Sign-In Dependency**:

```
yaml

dependencies:
  google_sign_in: ^5.0.7
```

2. **Sign In with Google**: Example of how to sign in using Google OAuth:

```
dart

import 'package:flutter/material.dart';
import
'package:google_sign_in/google_sign_in.da
rt';

class AuthService {
  final GoogleSignIn _googleSignIn =
GoogleSignIn();

  Future<void> signInWithGoogle() async {
    try {
      GoogleSignInAccount? account = await
_googleSignIn.signIn();
      if (account != null) {
```

```
        print('Signed        in        as:
${account.displayName}');
      }
    } catch (error) {
      print('Error during Google sign-in:
$error');
    }
  }

  Future<void> signOut() async {
    await _googleSignIn.signOut();
  }
}
```

Using Flutter's Secure Storage

When it comes to securely storing sensitive data like tokens, passwords, and other user information, Flutter provides the **flutter_secure_storage** package, which uses platform-specific secure storage solutions (iOS Keychain and Android Keystore) to store data securely.

Setting Up Secure Storage:

1. **Add flutter_secure_storage Dependency**:

```
yaml
```

```
dependencies:
  flutter_secure_storage: ^5.0.2
```

2. **Store and Retrieve Data**: Example of using `flutter_secure_storage` to securely store a JWT token:

```
dart

import
'package:flutter_secure_storage/flutter_secure_
storage.dart';

class SecureStorageService {
  final     FlutterSecureStorage     _storage     =
FlutterSecureStorage();

  // Store the JWT token
  Future<void> storeToken(String token) async {
    await    _storage.write(key:    'jwt_token',
value: token);
  }

  // Retrieve the JWT token
  Future<String?> getToken() async {
    return        await        _storage.read(key:
'jwt_token');
  }
```

```
  // Delete the JWT token
  Future<void> deleteToken() async {
    await _storage.delete(key: 'jwt_token');
  }
}
```

How Secure Storage Works:

- **iOS**: Uses the iOS Keychain to store data.
- **Android**: Uses the Android Keystore to store data. Both solutions ensure that sensitive data is stored in a secure, encrypted manner, protecting it from unauthorized access.

Real-World Example: Building a Secure Login System with JWT

Let's build a simple login system that uses **JWT** for authentication and **flutter_secure_storage** for securely storing the token.

Step 1: Set Up the App UI

Create a simple login UI where users can enter their credentials.

```
dart

import 'package:flutter/material.dart';
```

```
void main() {
  runApp(MyApp());
}

class MyApp extends StatelessWidget {
  @override
  Widget build(BuildContext context) {
    return MaterialApp(
      home: LoginScreen(),
    );
  }
}

class LoginScreen extends StatefulWidget {
  @override
  _LoginScreenState        createState()        =>
_LoginScreenState();
}

class          _LoginScreenState          extends
State<LoginScreen> {
  final          _usernameController          =
TextEditingController();
  final          _passwordController          =
TextEditingController();

  void _login() {
    //  Here  we  will  implement  the  login
functionality
```

```
  }

  @override
  Widget build(BuildContext context) {
    return Scaffold(
      appBar:     AppBar(title:     Text('Secure
Login')),
      body: Padding(
        padding: const EdgeInsets.all(16.0),
        child: Column(
          children: [
            TextField(
              controller: _usernameController,
              decoration:
InputDecoration(labelText: 'Username'),
            ),
            TextField(
              controller: _passwordController,
              decoration:
InputDecoration(labelText: 'Password'),
              obscureText: true,
            ),
            ElevatedButton(
              onPressed: _login,
              child: Text('Login'),
            ),
          ],
        ),
      ),
```

```
    );
  }
}
```

Step 2: Implementing the Login Functionality

In the `_login()` function, you will authenticate the user by sending their credentials to the server. If the login is successful, you will receive a JWT token.

```
dart

import 'package:http/http.dart' as http;
import 'dart:convert';
import
'package:flutter_secure_storage/flutter_secure_
storage.dart';

class AuthService {
  final         String         apiUrl         =
'https://example.com/api/login';
  final    FlutterSecureStorage    _storage    =
FlutterSecureStorage();

  Future<void>  login(String  username,  String
password) async {
    final response = await http.post(
      Uri.parse(apiUrl),
```

```
      body:  json.encode({'username':  username,
'password': password}),
      headers:                    {'Content-Type':
'application/json'},
    );

    if (response.statusCode == 200) {
      var data = json.decode(response.body);
      String token = data['token'];  // JWT token

      // Store the token securely
      await   _storage.write(key:   'jwt_token',
value: token);
      print('Logged in successfully');
    } else {
      throw Exception('Failed to login');
    }
  }
}
```

Step 3: Securely Storing the Token

After a successful login, we store the JWT token using `flutter_secure_storage` to keep the user authenticated across app sessions.

```
dart

Future<void> storeToken(String token) async {
```

```
  await _storage.write(key: 'jwt_token', value:
token);
}

Future<String?> getToken() async {
  return await _storage.read(key: 'jwt_token');
}

Future<void> deleteToken() async {
  await _storage.delete(key: 'jwt_token');
}
```

Step 4: Accessing the Token

To authenticate API requests, retrieve the token from secure storage and include it in the HTTP headers.

```
dart

Future<void> fetchData() async {
  String? token = await _storage.read(key:
'jwt_token');
  if (token != null) {
    final response = await http.get(
      Uri.parse('https://example.com/protected-
resource'),
      headers: {
        'Authorization': 'Bearer $token',
        'Content-Type': 'application/json'
```

```
      },
    );

    if (response.statusCode == 200) {
      print('Data: ${response.body}');
    } else {
      print('Failed to fetch data');
    }
  }
}
```

Conclusion

In this chapter, we explored how to secure user data and implement secure authentication in Flutter apps. We discussed how to implement **JWT authentication** for secure login, how to securely store tokens using **flutter_secure_storage**, and how to protect sensitive information. By using secure authentication methods like JWT and OAuth, along with secure storage techniques, you can ensure that your Flutter apps meet industry-standard security practices. In the next chapter, we will explore testing strategies for ensuring your app's security and reliability.

CHAPTER 25

BUILDING MULTI-LANGUAGE (INTERNATIONALIZED) APPS

Introduction to Internationalization (i18n) and Localization (l10n)

When building apps for global users, **internationalization (i18n)** and **localization (l10n)** are crucial concepts. These practices ensure that your app can be adapted to different languages, regions, and cultural norms without requiring extensive rework for each language.

What is Internationalization (i18n)?

Internationalization refers to the process of designing your app so that it can be easily adapted to multiple languages and regions. This involves abstracting any text, images, and other culture-specific content, making it easy to change for different locales without altering the app's core functionality.

For example, internationalization might include setting up your app to:

- Accept different character sets (e.g., Latin, Arabic, Chinese).
- Display dates, times, numbers, and currencies in a region-specific format.
- Handle right-to-left (RTL) languages like Arabic and Hebrew.

What is Localization (l10n)?

Localization is the process of adapting your app to a specific language and region after internationalization has been done. This includes:

- Translating text into the target language.
- Adjusting UI components for text direction (LTR vs. RTL).
- Formatting dates, times, numbers, and currencies according to the region.

In summary:

- **Internationalization** (i18n) prepares your app for localization.
- **Localization** (l10n) is the actual translation and cultural adaptation for a specific region.

Setting Up Multiple Languages in Flutter

Flutter provides a built-in package called `flutter_localizations` that allows you to internationalize and localize your app. To enable this functionality, you need to set up locale-specific resources such as language files and translation assets.

Steps to Set Up Localization in Flutter:

1. **Add Dependencies**: In your `pubspec.yaml` file, add the `flutter_localizations` package along with the localization support packages:

   ```
   yaml

   dependencies:
     flutter:
       sdk: flutter
     flutter_localizations:
       sdk: flutter
   ```

2. **Configure the Supported Locales**: Flutter allows you to specify which locales your app supports. Add this configuration in the `MaterialApp` widget.

   Example:

   ```
   dart
   ```

```
import 'package:flutter/material.dart';
import
'package:flutter_localizations/flutter_lo
calizations.dart';

void main() {
  runApp(MyApp());
}

class MyApp extends StatelessWidget {
  @override
  Widget build(BuildContext context) {
    return MaterialApp(
      title: 'Flutter Localization',
      supportedLocales: [
        Locale('en', 'US'), // English
        Locale('es', 'ES'), // Spanish
        Locale('fr', 'FR'), // French
        Locale('de', 'DE'), // German
      ],
      localizationsDelegates: [

GlobalMaterialLocalizations.delegate,

GlobalWidgetsLocalizations.delegate,

GlobalCupertinoLocalizations.delegate,
      ],
```

```
        home: HomeScreen(),
      );
    }
  }

class HomeScreen extends StatelessWidget {
  @override
  Widget build(BuildContext context) {
    return Scaffold(
      appBar: AppBar(
        title:          Text('Localization
Example'),
      ),
      body: Center(
        child: Text(
          'Hello World', // This will be
translated based on locale
        ),
      ),
    );
  }
}
```

In this example:

- The `supportedLocales` list specifies the languages your app supports (English, Spanish, French, and German).

- The `localizationsDelegates` list adds the necessary delegates for localizing material widgets and other Flutter components.

3. **Create Language Files**: To manage translations, you can create a `lib/l10n/` directory to store your locale-specific files. These files usually contain mappings of keys to text in different languages.

Example `lib/l10n/intl_en.arb` file (for English):

```json
json

{
  "helloWorld": "Hello World"
}
```

Example `lib/l10n/intl_es.arb` file (for Spanish):

```json
json

{
  "helloWorld": "Hola Mundo"
}
```

4. **Generate Dart Files**: Flutter has a tool called `flutter_localizations` that converts `.arb` files into Dart files that Flutter can use to fetch localized values.

You can use the `intl` package to automate this process. Add the `intl` and `intl_translation` dependencies in your `pubspec.yaml` file:

```
yaml

dependencies:
  flutter:
    sdk: flutter
  intl: ^0.17.0

dev_dependencies:
  intl_translation: ^0.17.10
```

Then, generate the Dart files using the `flutter_localizations` tool.

Handling Date, Time, and Currency in Different Locales

In addition to text, Flutter allows you to handle region-specific formatting for things like dates, times, numbers, and currencies.

Formatting Date and Time:

Flutter's `intl` package allows you to format dates and times according to different locales.

```
dart

import 'package:intl/intl.dart';

void main() {
  var date = DateTime.now();
  var formattedDate =
DateFormat.yMd().format(date);
  print(formattedDate); // Outputs: 12/1/2021
(in US locale)
}
```

The `DateFormat.yMd()` uses the default locale for formatting, but you can specify a custom locale:

```
dart

var formattedDate =
DateFormat.yMd('es_ES').format(date);
print(formattedDate); // Outputs: 01/12/2021 (in
Spanish locale)
```

Handling Currency:

To format currencies in different locales, you can use `NumberFormat`.

```
dart
```

```
import 'package:intl/intl.dart';

void main() {
  var number = 1234567.89;
  var formattedCurrency =
NumberFormat.simpleCurrency(locale:
'en_US').format(number);
  print(formattedCurrency); // Outputs:
$1,234,567.89
}
```

You can change the locale to `fr_FR` or `es_ES` for French or Spanish formatting, respectively:

```
dart

var formattedCurrency =
NumberFormat.simpleCurrency(locale:
'es_ES').format(number);
print(formattedCurrency); // Outputs:
1.234.567,89 €
```

Handling Numbers:

You can also format numbers according to the locale using the `NumberFormat` class.

```
dart
```

```
var    formattedNumber    =    NumberFormat('#,###',
'en_US').format(1234567);
print(formattedNumber); // Outputs: 1,234,567
```

Real-World Example: Creating a Multi-Language App

Let's build a simple multi-language app that displays a welcome message in different languages based on the selected locale. We will also format the date and currency according to the user's locale.

Step 1: Create Translation Files

Create the following `.arb` files in the `lib/l10n/` directory:

intl_en.arb (English):

```
json

{
  "welcome":  "Welcome  to  the  Multi-Language
App!",
  "date": "Today is {date}",
  "currency": "Price: {price}"
}
```

intl_es.arb (Spanish):

json

```
{
  "welcome": "¡Bienvenido a la Aplicación Multilenguaje!",
  "date": "Hoy es {date}",
  "currency": "Precio: {price}"
}
```

Step 2: Implement the App UI

Use the `Intl.message()` method to fetch localized strings in your Flutter app.

dart

```
import 'package:flutter/material.dart';
import 'package:intl/intl.dart';
import 'package:intl/intl.dart';

void main() {
  runApp(MyApp());
}

class MyApp extends StatelessWidget {
  @override
  Widget build(BuildContext context) {
    return MaterialApp(
      supportedLocales: [
```

```
        Locale('en', 'US'), // English
        Locale('es', 'ES'), // Spanish
      ],
      localizationsDelegates: [
        GlobalMaterialLocalizations.delegate,
        GlobalWidgetsLocalizations.delegate,
        GlobalCupertinoLocalizations.delegate,
      ],
      home: HomeScreen(),
    );
  }
}

class HomeScreen extends StatelessWidget {
  @override
  Widget build(BuildContext context) {
    final                locale                =
Localizations.localeOf(context);

    // Fetch the welcome message
    String welcomeMessage = Intl.message(
      'Welcome to the Multi-Language App!',
      name: 'welcome',
      locale: locale.toString(),
    );

    // Format date and currency based on locale
    var date = DateTime.now();
```

```
    var formattedDate =
DateFormat.yMd(locale.toString()).format(date);
    var number = 1234567.89;
    var formattedCurrency =
NumberFormat.simpleCurrency(locale:
locale.toString()).format(number);

    return Scaffold(
      appBar: AppBar(title:
Text(welcomeMessage)),
      body: Padding(
        padding: const EdgeInsets.all(16.0),
        child: Column(
          children: <Widget>[
            Text(welcomeMessage, style:
TextStyle(fontSize: 24)),
            SizedBox(height: 20),
            Text('Date: $formattedDate', style:
TextStyle(fontSize: 20)),
            SizedBox(height: 20),
            Text('Price: $formattedCurrency',
style: TextStyle(fontSize: 20)),
          ],
        ),
      ),
    );
  }
}
```

Explanation:

- The app supports **English** and **Spanish** locales.
- The localized strings for the welcome message, date, and currency are displayed according to the selected locale.
- The app uses `Intl.message()` to fetch the appropriate translations and formats the date and currency using `DateFormat` and `NumberFormat`.

Conclusion

In this chapter, we explored how to build multi-language apps in Flutter using **internationalization (i18n)** and **localization (l10n)**. We learned how to:

- Set up multiple languages and manage translations using `.arb` files.
- Handle locale-specific data such as dates, times, and currencies.
- Create a real-world example of a multi-language app with dynamic locale switching, date, and currency formatting.

By following these steps, you can make your Flutter apps accessible to a global audience, providing an excellent user experience in different languages and regions. In the next chapter, we will explore app performance optimization techniques to ensure your app runs efficiently on all devices.

CHAPTER 26

MAINTAINING AND SCALING FLUTTER APPS

Scaling Flutter Apps for Larger User Bases

As your Flutter app grows and attracts more users, scaling becomes an essential consideration to maintain smooth performance and responsiveness. Whether it's scaling the user interface, managing app data, or optimizing server-side resources, it's crucial to plan ahead to ensure that your app can handle a larger number of users.

Key Strategies for Scaling Flutter Apps:

1. **Optimizing Performance**:
   - **Efficient Rendering**: Use widgets like `ListView.builder` and `GridView.builder` to render only the visible items on the screen. This avoids memory overhead caused by rendering large datasets.
   - **Image and Asset Optimization**: Use appropriately sized images and assets to reduce memory usage. You can use the

`cached_network_image` package to cache images and prevent unnecessary downloads.

 - **Asynchronous Operations**: Offload resource-intensive tasks (like API calls, database queries, etc.) to background threads to prevent blocking the main thread and causing jank.

2. **Use Lazy Loading**: Implement lazy loading techniques for lists and other components. This means loading data only when it's needed (e.g., when the user scrolls to the end of a list).

   Example:

```dart
dart

ListView.builder(
  itemCount: items.length,
  itemBuilder: (context, index) {
    return ListTile(
      title: Text(items[index]),
    );
  },
);
```

3. **Caching Data**: Use local storage mechanisms like SQLite or `shared_preferences` to cache data locally and reduce server load, especially for frequently accessed

resources. This is particularly useful for apps that require real-time updates or handle large datasets.

4. **Load Balancing**: For backend services, implement **load balancing** to distribute incoming requests across multiple servers, ensuring that no single server becomes overloaded as traffic increases.

Managing App Data and Offline Support

One of the key challenges in mobile app development is managing data, especially when the app needs to work offline. Flutter provides several options for managing data both online and offline.

Offline Support in Flutter:

1. **Caching Data Locally**: Use databases like **SQLite** or the **Hive** database to store data on the device when the app is offline. You can then sync this data with your server when the user comes online.

   Example using **Hive**:

   ```
   yaml

   dependencies:
   ```

```
  hive: ^2.0.0
  hive_flutter: ^1.0.0
  path_provider: ^2.0.0
```

After setting up Hive, you can store and retrieve data easily:

```
dart

var box = await Hive.openBox('dataBox');
box.put('user', 'John Doe');
String user = box.get('user');
```

2. **Syncing Data with the Server**: For apps that work offline, it's essential to sync local data with the server when the device is back online. Flutter supports background services using packages like **workmanager** to periodically sync data or perform other tasks.

   Example using **workmanager**:

```
dart

import
'package:workmanager/workmanager.dart';

void syncData() {
  // Code to sync local data with the
server
```

```
}

void main() {
  runApp(MyApp());

Workmanager().initialize(callbackDispatch
er);
}

void callbackDispatcher() {
  Workmanager().executeTask((task,
inputData) {
    syncData();
    return Future.value(true);
  });
}
```

3. **Handling Data Conflicts**: When syncing data, conflicts may arise between local and remote data. Implement strategies such as **last-write-wins** or **merge strategies** to resolve conflicts and maintain consistency between the client and server.

Continuous Integration and Continuous Deployment (CI/CD)

CI/CD is a software development practice that automates the process of building, testing, and deploying your app. This is critical for ensuring high-quality, bug-free releases and reducing the manual effort in maintaining the app. By setting up a CI/CD pipeline, you can ensure that every change in your codebase is automatically tested, built, and deployed.

Setting Up CI/CD for Flutter Apps:

1. **CI/CD Tools**: Several tools can help set up CI/CD pipelines for Flutter apps. Some popular choices include:
   - **GitHub Actions**
   - **Bitrise**
   - **Codemagic**
   - **CircleCI**
2. **GitHub Actions for Flutter**: GitHub Actions is a powerful tool for automating workflows directly within your GitHub repository. Here's an example of setting up a GitHub Actions workflow for Flutter:
   1. Create a `.github/workflows/flutter.yml` file in your repository.
   2. Add the following content to set up the workflow:

```
yaml

name: Flutter CI

on:
  push:
    branches:
```

```
      - main

jobs:
  build:
    runs-on: ubuntu-latest

    steps:
      - name: Checkout code
        uses: actions/checkout@v2

      - name: Set up Flutter
        uses: subosito/flutter-action@v2
        with:
          flutter-version: '2.5.0'

      - name: Install dependencies
        run: flutter pub get

      - name: Run tests
        run: flutter test

      - name: Build APK
        run: flutter build apk --release

      - name: Build iOS
        run: flutter build ios --release
```

In this setup:

- **`flutter pub get`** installs dependencies.

    - `flutter test` runs the unit tests.
    - `flutter build apk` builds a release version of the Android app.
    - `flutter build ios` builds a release version of the iOS app.
3. **Automated Testing**: Set up automated testing within your CI/CD pipeline to run unit tests, widget tests, and integration tests automatically with each build. This ensures that any new changes don't introduce bugs.
4. **Deploy to App Stores**: For automating deployments, you can set up deployment scripts to automatically publish the app to the Google Play Store or Apple App Store after a successful build.

   For **Google Play**, you can use **fastlane** to automate the release process.

Real-World Example: Scaling an E-commerce App Built with Flutter

Let's walk through an example of how you might scale an e-commerce app built with Flutter to handle an increasing number of users and data.

Step 1: Optimize the UI:

1. **Lazy Loading of Products**: Instead of loading all products at once, you can use a `ListView.builder` to load products dynamically as the user scrolls.
2. **Optimizing Images**: Use the `cached_network_image` package to cache images, reducing network requests and improving performance.

```dart
CachedNetworkImage(
  imageUrl: product.imageUrl,
  placeholder:     (context,     url)     =>
CircularProgressIndicator(),
)
```

Step 2: Implement Offline Support:

1. **Caching Product Data**: Store the product data in a local database like SQLite or Hive so that the app can continue to function when offline.
2. **Sync Data in the Background**: Use the `workmanager` package to sync the user's cart or order data with the backend server when the device is online.

Step 3: CI/CD Setup:

Set up a CI/CD pipeline (using GitHub Actions or Codemagic) to automatically test, build, and deploy the e-commerce app. This ensures that every new feature or bug fix is automatically tested and deployed to the app stores.

Step 4: Load Balancing and Backend Scaling:

As the user base grows, you'll need to scale your backend infrastructure:

1. **Database Scaling**: Use a cloud-based database (e.g., Firebase Firestore, PostgreSQL) with automatic scaling to handle a large volume of transactions.
2. **Server Scaling**: Implement load balancing and auto-scaling for your servers to distribute the user load efficiently.

Conclusion

In this chapter, we covered key strategies for maintaining and scaling Flutter apps. We discussed how to scale your app to handle more users by optimizing performance, managing data both online and offline, and setting up CI/CD pipelines for continuous testing and deployment. We also looked at a real-world example of scaling an e-commerce app, from implementing offline support to optimizing the backend. With the right practices and tools, you can ensure that your Flutter apps grow efficiently and handle increased user demands seamlessly. In the next chapter, we will explore best practices for managing app security and ensuring that your app is robust and safe for users.

CHAPTER 27

THE FUTURE OF FLUTTER AND MOBILE APP DEVELOPMENT

What's Next for Flutter: Upcoming Features

Flutter is constantly evolving, with new features and improvements being added to enhance performance, developer experience, and cross-platform capabilities. In this section, we'll explore some of the exciting features that are expected to shape the future of Flutter and mobile app development.

Upcoming Features in Flutter:

1. **Flutter 3 and Beyond**: With the release of **Flutter 3**, the framework introduced several features aimed at improving performance, supporting additional platforms, and enhancing the development experience.

   Key features include:

   - **Improved support for macOS, Linux, and Windows**: Flutter is becoming increasingly capable as a desktop framework, with native desktop support becoming more stable and feature-rich.

- **Web Improvements**: Flutter for Web continues to improve, with optimizations in rendering performance and the ability to use Flutter's tooling for production-level web apps.
- **Dart DevTools Enhancements**: New debugging, profiling, and performance tools are added, allowing for even more efficient debugging and testing in Flutter apps.

2. **Flutter DevTools Updates**: Flutter's suite of development tools, **DevTools**, is expected to continue evolving with more powerful features for debugging, performance profiling, and hot-reloading across platforms.
3. **Flutter for Embedded Systems**: As part of its ongoing expansion, Flutter is increasingly being used for **embedded systems** like automotive UIs, smart displays, and IoT devices. Flutter is being adapted for a broader range of devices, opening new possibilities for developers.
4. **New Platform Support**: Flutter will continue to introduce support for new platforms such as **TVOS**, **WearOS**, and **Fuchsia**. With these additions, Flutter is becoming a true cross-platform development tool,

extending its capabilities to a wider range of devices beyond mobile and desktop.

5. **Improved Null Safety**: Null safety is one of Dart's most anticipated features. While it's already available, Flutter will continue to improve its integration with null safety, making apps more robust and reducing runtime errors.

Evolving Mobile Development Trends

Mobile app development is a fast-evolving space, with new technologies and trends shaping the way apps are built. As mobile apps become increasingly complex, developers need to keep up with emerging trends to stay competitive and build the best user experiences.

Key Trends in Mobile App Development:

1. **Cross-Platform Development**: Cross-platform frameworks like Flutter, React Native, and Xamarin continue to grow in popularity. These frameworks allow developers to write a single codebase for both Android and iOS, reducing development time and costs.
    - **Flutter**: Flutter is leading the cross-platform charge, with its hot reload capabilities, extensive widget library, and growing community support.

   - **React Native**: React Native remains a strong contender, with Facebook's backing and a huge ecosystem of libraries.
2. **5G and Mobile Connectivity**: The rollout of **5G networks** will significantly impact mobile development. With higher speeds and lower latency, apps will become more data-intensive and real-time, providing opportunities for developers to create more immersive and interactive experiences.
3. **Augmented Reality (AR) and Virtual Reality (VR)**: Mobile devices are becoming increasingly capable of supporting **AR and VR** experiences. Flutter is working towards integrating AR and VR tools into the framework, allowing developers to build immersive experiences for games, shopping, education, and more.
4. **AI and Machine Learning**: AI and **machine learning** are becoming essential components of mobile apps. From smart assistants to recommendation systems, mobile apps will continue integrating AI to enhance user experiences. Flutter is incorporating more integrations with machine learning models, such as TensorFlow Lite, to enable these features.
5. **Mobile Payments and Wallets**: Mobile wallets and payment systems, including **Apple Pay**, **Google Pay**, and **cryptocurrency wallets**, are becoming mainstream. Developers are increasingly focusing on integrating

secure and easy-to-use payment systems into their mobile apps.

Building Progressive Web Apps with Flutter

Flutter is not just for mobile app development—it also has great potential for creating **Progressive Web Apps (PWAs)**. PWAs are web apps that provide a mobile-app-like experience using the web browser. They offer benefits like offline support, push notifications, and the ability to be installed on the home screen, making them a powerful alternative to traditional apps.

Why Choose Flutter for PWAs?

1. **Single Codebase**: With Flutter's cross-platform capabilities, you can use the same codebase to build both mobile and web apps. This is particularly useful for creating **PWAs**, as you don't have to manage separate codebases for web and mobile versions of the app.
2. **Fast Performance**: Flutter for Web continues to improve, offering smooth performance for PWAs. With Flutter's native compilation and high-performance rendering engine, your PWA can have an app-like feel with fast load times and seamless user interactions.

3. **Customizable UI**: Flutter's rich set of customizable widgets makes it easy to create beautiful and responsive PWAs that adapt well to various screen sizes, from mobile phones to desktops.
4. **Offline Support**: One of the core features of PWAs is offline capability, and Flutter makes it easy to implement this by caching resources and data using service workers and local storage.
5. **Native-Like Experience**: PWAs built with Flutter can provide a native app experience, including features like push notifications, offline functionality, and access to device hardware.

Steps to Create a PWA with Flutter:

1. **Set Up a Flutter Web Project**: Ensure that you have Flutter 2.x or above, as Flutter has added stable support for web development. Run:

   ```
   bash

   flutter create my_pwa_app
   cd my_pwa_app
   flutter run -d chrome
   ```

2. **Add PWA Support**: Use the `flutter build web` command to generate the necessary files for PWA support, including a manifest and service worker. In your

project's `web/` directory, update the `index.html` to include the necessary meta tags for PWA features.

3. **Enable Offline Support**: Use service workers to cache assets and enable offline usage. Flutter handles this automatically for web builds, but you may want to customize it based on your app's needs.
4. **Deploy Your PWA**: After building your Flutter app for the web, deploy it to a web server that supports HTTPS. PWAs require HTTPS for functionality like service workers and push notifications.

How to Stay Updated and Continue Learning

The mobile app development ecosystem is continuously evolving, and it's essential to stay updated on the latest trends, best practices, and tools. Here are some ways to keep learning and growing as a Flutter developer:

1. **Official Flutter Documentation**: The official Flutter documentation is a comprehensive resource for learning and exploring new features in Flutter. It includes tutorials, guides, and API references.
    - Flutter Docs
2. **Community and Forums**: The Flutter community is large and active, with many developers sharing insights,

solutions, and tutorials. Engaging with the community via forums, Discord channels, and Stack Overflow is a great way to learn from others.

   - Flutter Community

3. **Attend Meetups and Conferences**: Join Flutter meetups, conferences, and events to network with other developers, learn new techniques, and get inspired by real-world use cases and innovations.
4. **Follow Blogs and Podcasts**: Many developers and tech influencers regularly share their knowledge through blogs and podcasts. Some popular blogs and podcasts to follow include:
   - FlutterDev Medium
   - The Flutter Podcast
5. **Keep Experimenting**: The best way to learn is through hands-on experience. Experiment with new features in Flutter, explore different libraries, and try building unique projects to hone your skills.

Real-World Example: Exploring the Future of Cross-Platform Development

Let's consider an example of building a **cross-platform e-commerce app** using Flutter that leverages Flutter's capabilities for mobile, web, and desktop. The app needs to provide a seamless shopping experience on mobile devices, desktops, and as a Progressive Web App (PWA).

Steps Involved:

1. **Mobile App (Flutter)**: The e-commerce app is built with Flutter for both iOS and Android, featuring a responsive UI and fast performance.
2. **Web App (Flutter for Web)**: The same codebase is used to build a web version of the app. It supports all the features found in the mobile app and can be accessed in a browser as a PWA, allowing users to install it on their home screen for offline support.
3. **Desktop App (Flutter Desktop)**: The desktop version of the app is built using Flutter's growing support for macOS, Windows, and Linux. Users can access the app on their computers for a more immersive shopping experience.
4. **Backend Integration**: The app integrates with a backend (e.g., Firebase, REST API) to manage user authentication, product data, and orders.
5. **Payment Integration**: The app integrates payment gateways like **Stripe** for handling secure payments.
6. **CI/CD Pipeline**: The app is built and tested using CI/CD pipelines, ensuring quick releases and updates across all platforms.

Conclusion

In this chapter, we explored the exciting future of Flutter and mobile app development. We discussed the upcoming features in Flutter, the evolving trends in mobile development, and how Flutter is being used to build Progressive Web Apps (PWAs). Additionally, we learned how to stay updated with the latest advancements in Flutter development. The real-world example of building a cross-platform e-commerce app demonstrated how Flutter can be used to create seamless, high-quality apps for mobile, web, and desktop platforms. Flutter's ability to target multiple platforms with a single codebase continues to make it a powerful tool for developers. As Flutter evolves, its cross-platform capabilities will only continue to grow, making it one of the best choices for mobile and web development.

www.ingramcontent.com/pod-product-compliance
Lightning Source LLC
LaVergne TN
LVHW022333060326
832902LV00022B/4013
9798280361003